TILLER'S GIRLS

DOREMY VERNON

Robson Books

First published in Great Britain in 1988 by Robson Books Ltd,
Bolsover House, 5 – 6 Clipstone Street, London W1P 7EB.

British Library Cataloguing in Publication Data

Vernon, Doremy
   Tiller's girls.
   1. Dancing. Tiller Girls
   I. Title
   793.3'2

ISBN 0-86051-480-3

Typeset in Great Britain by JCL Graphics, Bristol

Printed in Great Britain at the University Printing House,
Oxford by David Stanford

Contents

1 A Lancashire Lad's Way to Fame and Fortune 9

2 Blackpool Children Get Their Chance 24

3 How John Retrieves a Lost Fortune, But Loses a Son 42

4 'A Pound for Me Mum . . .' 56

5 'Paris, of Course' 72

6 'We Were the Cream de la Crême' 91

7 'The Mrs Carries On' 104

8 'Will There Be Food?' 116

9 'Send Me Where I'll Be Most Useful' 128

10 'What's Happening?' 144

11 Finale — Wipe 159

Acknowledgements

To all Tiller Girls who let me share their memories. Special thanks too, to the following who believed in my dream that this book would be published. Mary Atthey, Bernard Crabtree, Edwina Dorman, Denbry Repros, Marjorie Dubber, Marjorie Fairley, Jimmy Gilmour, Leslie Hallihan, Barrie Houghton, Brian Ingham, Miles Kreuger (Institute of the American Musical), Geoff J. Mellor, Stanley Miller, Wilf Parkin and the Manchester Music Hall Society, Susan Rea, Loesje Sanders, the late Robert J. Smith. Also Diana Miller, without whom I never would have appeared on stage and Pam Harcourt who brought us all together again.

Unless otherwise specified, the majority of photographs come from the author's collection or are kindly supplied by the Tiller Girls themselves.

Preface

'IT WAS A nice dream but if I really think about it, a blooming hard slog.' These words were said by Patricia Walker, a Tiller Girl in the early 1960s. The feelings behind them have been echoed countless times by women who danced in the troupes.

I interviewed over 200 Girls before compiling this book. It was not my intention to explode any myths, to push any pedestals. I simply report their thoughts. I thank all of them for collaborating with me. I dedicate the book to all Tiller Girls everywhere, in fact to all dancers. They are sometimes exploited, indeed often allow themselves to be exploited, in order to fulfil their dream of dancing and give the public entertainment.

I give you the Tiller Girls.

DOREMY VERNON

1

A Lancashire Lad's Way to Fame and Fortune

'I WAS A Tiller Girl.'
If you are eligible to say that, anyone over the age of forty will be impressed in the nicest possible way. Usually dancers are leered at or looked down on whenever they mention their job, so why are Tiller Girls different?

It is extraordinary that their image of being hardworking, respectable and down-to-earth has lasted for so many years. So strong are the memories of the Girls that whenever they announce a reunion, photographers and journalists are eager to record the event.

How many women can claim to have been a Tiller Girl? It certainly runs into thousands. And it all began in 1890 when a successful businessman, who could not dance a step, presented four ordinary little girls from Manchester in a pantomime at the Prince of Wales Theatre, Liverpool. All over the country children worked in similar acts but this particular quartet, *Les Jolies Petites,* was fortunate. Their mentor was brilliant at his job. His name was John Tiller.

A standing ovation greeted the end of their encore on the opening night and such praise was lavished on the troupe during the run that Tiller resolved to give up his work in the cotton trade and throw in his lot with the theatrical profession. He was thirty-six years old and had heavy family commitments; it was late in life to change course, but he had hankered after the theatre for years and now decided to follow his instincts. He might have had thoughts of destiny but it is unlikely that even he could conceive that troupes of girls bearing his name would still be dancing nearly a hundred years later.

His true parentage was kept secret even from most of his family. Far from having a rich father, he was the illegitimate son of Maria Frances Tiller, born in Blackburn on 13th June, 1854, when his mother was twenty-four years old. The father was not named at the registration of birth; but maybe his mother took revenge on him when she added an unusual Christian name, Ibbotson, to follow the two commonplace forenames, John and Thomas.

The stark, blank space in the column listing 'father's name and occupation' on his birth certificate was to haunt him all his life. He and his mother were to become defiant of officialdom and simply falsified information on official forms whenever they wanted.

When John was ten, he became a choirboy. His ambition, which was to drive him so hard in later life, resulted in his being made choirmaster by the time he was fourteen — his first taste of authority. His deep love of music moved him to take lessons with Dr Hiles, (later Professor of

Harmony and Composition at the Royal Northern College of Music) and the young Tiller showed an early flair by winning prizes for harmony while studying under him.

In 1872 his mother married a joiner called William Pointon. By that time Maria was forty-two and her bridegroom only thirty-one, but with her usual disregard for red tape, she put down her age as thirty-three at the wedding ceremony. All her life she refused to give her true age even after her young husband left her.

A year after her marriage she had her second and last child, Frederick William. John himself was in no hurry to get married, he still lived with his mother in a small working man's house in Moss Side and enjoyed a good social life.

His uncle, John George, owned a highly successful cotton agency which was one of the largest in Manchester, and he had the wealthy lifestyle that his nephew craved. His enormous merchant's house was full of beautiful furniture, glass, china and musical instruments. Pictures and prints adorned his walls. Fourteen servants waited on the family. His stable contained not one but several carriages. Here John learned to appreciate the material things in life and in later years he allowed journalists to make the mistake of attributing John George's wealth and position to him at this time.

The well-to-do uncle treated John as a son and took him into his expanding business. He described himself as the 'natural son' of his parents on his baptism certificate, and this may explain the affinity he felt for the boy. During the day John worked in the cotton trade, and in his spare time he devoted his energy to music and various activities, such as acting as the secretary for cricket clubs, always with the intention of promoting his business career.

At nineteen, marriage was thrust upon him when one of his many girlfriends announced she was pregnant. Mary Carr was also nineteen. She was a shy, retiring girl, always overwhelmed by her forceful bridegroom with his immense appetite for life.

At their wedding ceremony on Christmas Eve, 1873, John took embarrassing matters into his own hands and nominated a Thomas Tiller as his father and claimed to be of full age. He certainly was in no hurry to marry poor Mary as she was already six and half months pregnant. The couple went to live with his mother. Soon the little terrace house became a hub of domestic activity when not only his first daughter Eleanor Elizabeth played with his half brother but they were joined two years later by his second daughter, Florence.

More children came with monotonous regularity; within eleven years a total of ten children were born (of whom three did not survive). The eldest boy was endowed with the family name of John and the over-high expectations that the family had for their first sons. The relationship between father and son was always strained and the child insisted on having himself called by his second name, Lawrence, from quite an early age.

At this point John Tiller's business was promising. His uncle had entered him as a subscriber onto the Royal Exchange, Manchester, and made him a partner. The contrasting characters of John and Mary are clearly shown by the way each chose to describe his occupation when registering their children's births. While Mary relegated him to 'Manchester Warehouseman,' John preferred the more optimistic 'Cotton Manufacturer'! However, by 1884 even his timid wife believed in his

affluence as they had moved into a pleasant merchant's house in Didsbury where their youngest children, Walter and Jessie, were born.

His enjoyment of music now led him into more theatrical pursuits. He had become a stage manager and officer of the *Minnehaha Minstrels*. This was an enthusiastic amateur group, the members of which, all businessmen, would rehearse once a week in each other's houses and then, blackening their faces with burnt cork, perform for charities in the Manchester theatres. Whether their talent was as great as their enthusiasm is unlikely. One performer was a deaf flute player who had the habit of playing long after the others had finished. Whatever their standards, they were successful, collecting money for the charities whilst making good business contacts.

In 1885 John became director of the Comedy Theatre, Manchester, and in the same year he began teaching children to dance. His early pupils practised for hours every Saturday afternoon amongst the bales of cotton in one of the firm's warehouses. He also started to give lessons at his

Typical of the streets of Moss Side where most of the Tiller pupils came from. John lived in Granville Street from the age of 19. Number 8 not only housed his mother, her husband and son but John's wife and first four children stayed there too home, but his wife swiftly showed her disapproval. Already known to have a weakness for a pretty face, it was understandable that she worried now he chose to teach attractive young girls. In their first public appearances these pupils performed tableaux and dances in church pageants, which were popular in the 1880s. Then John made use of his position as director of the Comedy Theatre and arranged the children's dances in the pantomime. In later, more celebrated, times he would always acknowledge this as his first theatrical experience. It was in fact a humble beginning, for the cast was enormous and his crowd work was not exceptional; he received neither credit in the programme nor any mention in the press for his direction.

During the day things were not going well at work. There certainly was trouble at the mill. Although John was a partner every move was under his uncle's direction. His cousin Samuel was now old enough to join his father and take his place as heir to the business, and the two young men were never compatible. John George had long ceased to play the father to John: not only did he put his son first at all times, but his alcoholism made him extremely difficult to deal with. The atmosphere between the three personalities was electric and one day there was a violent quarrel. John stormed out and set up in business on his own. The rift between the two younger men never healed after that quarrel, and their families never spoke again.

John Tiller led a fragmented existence at this time. He carried on presenting dancers in an amateur capacity, but it was an activity that was taking up more time than he could afford. He could not accept all the offers that were made, for he had after all to keep his large family of seven children in the manner he had chosen. He was well placed in the cotton industry and it gave him a generous income; therefore it had to take precedence, but the monotony of arriving at the same place at the same time every day now bored him as much as had the mechanical frenzy of the bobbins when he arrived.

In the autumn of 1890 Tiller was asked to present a quartet of children at the Prince of Wales Theatre, Liverpool, in the pantomime *Robinson Crusoe,* subtitled *The Good Friday That Came On A Saturday.* From his pupils in Manchester, he chose four tiny girls aged about ten. Their names were Dolly Grey, Tessie Lomax, Cissy and Lily Smith. He was exact in his choice; not only did they have the same slender shape and were equal in height, but they were malleable too. They had to be. Relentlessly he made them repeat every movement and worked them for hours on end until they were perfectly in unison. Most evenings they were so exhausted they had to be carried home on their parents' shoulders.

They were the first of thousands of Tiller Girls who would feel like crawling home after rehearsals. Every movement had to be perfect. Every head had to turn simultaneously. One early Tiller remembers:

We often cried with pain. Our feet often became too sore and blistered to be put into shoes, so we walked home in our stockinged feet.

The sheet music published after the first quartet's appearance (The Raymond Mander & Joe Mitchenson Theatre Collection)

John's mother, Maria, who had often earned her living as a seamstress, made the lavish costumes; the cream-coloured dresses made up in a

To Miss Jessie De Gray

MAMMA'S BABEE

A LULLABY

ARRANGED BY

JOHN TILLER

SUNG WITH ENORMOUS SUCCESS BY "Les Jolies Petites" THE EXCELSIOR QUARTETTE

AND ALSO SUNG WITH GREAT SUCCESS BY "LA PETITE QUARTETTE" IN THE BURLESQUE OF "DARRY THE DAUNTLESS"

Price, 4/-

LONDON. H. BERESFORD, 62, BERNERS ST. OXFORD ST. W. AND AT BIRMINGHAM.

W.T. Stannard litho

pinafore smock style reaching just below the knee. Each wore a blue sash at hip level, a matching bonnet, silk stockings and black shoes with a buckle. Wearing quality materials like cashmere, they must have felt like princesses.

Their routine was not the high-kicking style that eventually made John's name. Each child cradled a doll dressed in red and their first song was a lullaby, arranged by John, called *Mamma's Babee*.

> Clap hands and clap hands till Dada comes home,
> Baby had gum drops though Mamma has none.
> Hush-a-bye baby, Dada is near,
> Mamma's a lady that's very clear.

John was so sure of an encore that he rehearsed the girls in a burlesque version of a quartet from the Gaiety Theatre in London, and in a later scene they performed a coconut dance — a long-established feature of theatre and street dance of the time.

They certainly had a protective manager in John Tiller but the little girls were overwhelmed by their new way of life. They were now thirty-odd miles away from the Manchester slums where they had been brought up, a distance that put them beyond the range of mobility of their families, who could not afford to visit them.

The law demanded that they attend school for the few hours they were not in the theatre, but time spent on education was minimal as the pantomime was so popular that there were matinées most days. The curtain went up at 2 pm, so the children had to arrive at the theatre at about 1.15 to get ready. The production lasted well over three hours, and then it was soon time to get ready for the evening performance.

A matron chaperoned them at all times, trekking them from digs to school, on to the theatre and finally back to their digs at night, the crocodile of children walking slower as the day progressed. Tiller was a stickler for cleanliness, so she was told to be strict in supervising their washing (for some this was as novel an experience as appearing on stage).

The pantomime continued for three months. It was a clockwork existence for the children, but the rapturous applause more than compensated for their tiredness at the end of the day. They were made to write home once a week, proudly enclosing copies of their glowing write-ups from the newspapers, hoping that a neighbour could be found to help out with any reading difficulties.

As a final honour, normally reserved for either managers or principal performers, the troupe were allowed a benefit performance. Gifts from colleagues in the show and admirers in the audience would be presented on stage. Gold-topped walking canes or cigarette cases were typical presents of the time; the girls received numerous bouquets, and (from the producer, Captain Wombwell) a gold brooch each. The entire box office receipts were normally given to the lucky artiste. This was to compensate in some way for the rather poor salaries. In this instance it is unlikely that the children received any financial reward. John's fee was his first professional one and would only just cover the expenses of presenting the act.

Once John Tiller made the decision to become a professional manager, his business acumen surfaced. He treated the benefit performance as a showcase for his work. He devised a special programme, teaching the girls a new song and dance called *The Little Gypsies* and this earned their usual

encore. He also added another number called *The Little Musicians,* which was performed by four slightly older children.

He gave two solos to girls who repaid him by becoming loyal workers for many years. Little Dollie Bell recited a sad ballad entitled *At the Stage Door.* The second soloist was billed as 'Bessie Cowan, aged 11, who will perform a sailor's hornpipe'. She was, in fact, Bessie Cohen, who later rose to fame as a music hall soloist. She had a more bohemian background than any other Tiller pupil. Her father had come from Lithuania and started working as a tailor's presser, then he ran a clothes shop in the parlour of his house in Strangeways. Bessie was at a strict Jewish school at the time of her début and was expelled publicly for appearing in the theatre.

After their pantomime season, *Les Jolies Petites* toured for a year at

The earliest photo of any group of Tiller Girls. Taken c.1891 it includes Bessie Cohen (second right) who later became a successful Music Hall soloist various dates all over the country, always getting an excellent reception. Their relatives were overjoyed that they could see them on stage when they returned to their home town in the summer for a couple of weeks at the prestigious new Palace of Varieties. Their popularity resulted in Tiller getting a request not only to train the children and arrange the ballets but also to present a quartette of 'lady' dancers for the 1891 pantomime *The Fair One with the Golden Locks* at the Comedy Theatre, Manchester.

He called this group the *Tiller Quartette* and the girls were Annie Johnson, Patti Bell, Madge Vernon and Amy Knott. Amy had had previous theatrical work and soon became one of his principals. In truth this troupe did not receive the idolatry that his juveniles had aroused the previous year, but they must have pulled up their silk stockings because when they went on tour later one reviewer did describe them as:

> ...a charming set of young ladies who shine out prominently as sprightly vocalists and dancers, whose contributions to the programme are received with much favour.

Two groups appeared: the *Tiller Ballet* and the *Tiller Combination of Eight Ladies*. The word 'ladies' often figured in John's description of his dancers. He was at great pains to ensure that the public did not associate his performers with the bad name that dancers usually had. It was to be the golden rule that no Tiller would have a hint of scandal about her: a difficult task for the pretty vivacious girls from the poor streets of Moss Side. Suddenly they were wearing expensive clothes on and off stage, taking cabs everywhere, men were showering them with gifts in an attempt just to be seen with them. It was difficult to keep their feet on the ground when they read about themselves in the newspapers:

> I am more than pleased to see the Tiller troupe remain. My good friends of masher persuasion are in seventh heaven when they have the opportunity of admiring eight pretty faces. Eight sylphlike forms and eight pairs of dainty, twinkling feet and ankles. The rest of mankind and womankind also admire the physical attractions of those maidens and are roused to enthusiasm by their perfect dancing. Of course we must have cartwheels and the maiden to whose lot it had fallen to perform this important feature of the dance so very neatly and prettily is recalled. Several bouquets were handed up and no doubt well received.
>
> Mr Tiller has a worldwide reputation as a manager and trainer of vocalists and terpischorean troupes and this one certainly does him credit. Sir, I don't think I'll go to the Grand next week, I'm getting susceptible and it's a bit bewildering when there are eight and all in one troupe.
>
> The Tiller troupe is a terrific turn. I should think so when there are eight fascinating female forms in it, turning, twisting, pirouetting and corkscrewing about the stage at any one time. It is enough to turn the brains of all the gilded youth of Hull.

John had improved the standard of girls in the line, while other dancers in the commercial theatre tended to be ragged. A Producer would simply form a scratch troupe and almost throw them on stage. A mixture of shapes and sizes often working next to each other — fat, thin, tall and small. An ambitious dancer would kick high above her head, desperate to be noticed, while beside her another might hardly bother to lift her leg.

Managers found it impossible to maintain discipline: if a girl found a man to keep her for a while, she would 'scarper' (disappear). Replaced by a stagestruck girl of fourteen, recruited locally, she would be superficially trained in a matter of hours by the Head Girl then, absolutely terrified out of her wits, be put on stage the same night to pacify the Producer, for having paid for eight costumes for a number, he usually insisted on eight bodies filling them, whether or not they knew the routine. If two girls applied for the job then the one whose shape filled the costume got the job. Even with a few days' rehearsal it was an unnerving experience. It was unknown for Tiller's dancers to scarper and his replacements would be thoroughly rehearsed rather than discredit him.

The Gaiety Girls were the most fêted troupe at this time. They had high opinions of their value on stage, which made them rather undisciplined. One was notorious for talking on stage, to the annoyance of the principals who were desperate to get the attention of the audience. Seymour Hicks, the famous singer, once became so infuriated that he stopped the orchestra in the middle of his song, turned to the girl and snapped, 'Dear Lady, shall you finish your story or shall I finish my song?' There was a stunned silence on stage and in the audience. She looked him straight in the eye and said, 'Do you know, dearie, it's a matter of the utmost indifference to me what you do.' Such strict training was given by Tiller that none of his dancers would have contemplated talking in the first place.

It may have been a glamorous enough life on stage and, despite the famous Tiller ethos, at the stage door, where the young lads who laid siege to the girls came to be known as Stage Door Johnnies. But behind the scenes it was a different story. Hardened professionals were disgusted by the so-called dressing rooms. A comedian of the time described them in *The Stage*:

Two dressing rooms, one for the gentlemen, one for the ladies, all beautifully decorated with cobwebs and dust, the accumulation of years and uncovered stone floors.

The room I shared with others had evidently been a cellar under the street. Water oozed out of the walls and as each night wore on, the heat distilled a fetid and poisonous atmosphere. Clothes laid briefly against the wall became wet. A pail of cold water for washing was set on the floor so that performers had to bend over to use it. A cupboard measuring six foot by six foot for the 'star' actress.

Outside these dressing rooms runs a corridor — in other words a haunt of rats — at the end of which there is a water closet which gives off the most terrible stench, enough to upset the stomach of any weak person. This is a specimen of our dressing rooms, but not by far the worst, as I know of one in the North of England where a corner of the floor is submerged in filth and water.

Tiller's child dancers could not offset the grim conditions backstage with an exciting nightlife as adult performers could. Obviously, no stranger was allowed to approach them after a performance, and certainly no gifts were to be accepted. They were whisked away from the theatre by an ever vigilant matron, who stood over them while they had their dreaded wash with cold water from the jug and basin in their room. They would tour all over the country for wages of a few shillings a week.

Their education suffered, naturally:

On Mondays you went to the nearest school. Not that you did much, you'd be going from class to class entertaining the kids with your dances and stories. They didn't believe the names of some of the acts; Dulcie Laing, the serio and legmania dancer, Mademoiselle Hilarius and her demon pig Tordaunt, so we used to do impersonations of them . . .

Every week we would have to adjust to new teachers; it made us adaptable but didn't do much for our education.

Then we'd come back to the digs, wash our hair, have a wash if we were lucky, then on to the theatre. We had two performances a night and a Saturday matinée as well . . .

We often had to sleep four to a bed. 'Top and Tail' we called it. We soon learnt to notice if a bed was pulled away from the wall. If it was, that meant there were livestock in the room and the landlady had done that to stop these things falling from the wall onto the blankets.

We would have to pack up everything carefully on a Saturday night and travel on a Sunday. It became terribly hard in the winter.

Tiller's organization was efficient and matrons were vetted strictly, but a few negligent ones did slip through:

There was one matron when I was eleven, who was horrible. Mr Tiller used to come to tea every Sunday but we were too frightened to tell him about anything. I always remember the custard was lovely on a Sunday, the rest of the week it was like water.

When we used to go out in the street, I would be on one side of the matron holding her arm, my sister on the other side doing the same. We used to say 'First we go up, then we go down' as we lifted her up and down . . . Behind her back we would say to each other, 'She's drunk again'. She used to get tight regularly.

It was hard to keep a juvenile troupe together for any length of time. Children had the unfortunate habit of growing too tall, whereupon they would be sacked so the few shillings earned were lost to a family that might well depend on them.

If a girl had two parents still at home, she had to get written permission from both of them before performing. Women were more eager than their husbands to sign the note. 'Let her go,' they might say, 'give her a chance to see the world, after all who is she going to meet round here?' Hardly diplomatic but the man was persuaded. Another favourite argument was the fact that the girls received training. It was like an apprenticeship, and such a thing was rare for girls.

Great store was set on the word 'training'. It proudly appeared on many programmes. 'The Lamp Scene in which 200 trained children appear' was typical.

Other fathers were often unemployed and jealous of a child bringing home a weekly wage: understandable if they had a daughter like Dolly Ashby:

I'd run all the way home, put it on the table and say, 'There you are, I'm better than you, our Dad!'

Many had a puritanical objection to stagework. Even when Martha Sissons was a hundred years old, her father's disapproval was her strongest memory:

I was always afraid of me father. If he had known I was on the stage, he'd have murdered me. So me mother used to keep it dark. It was the seven shillings wages I was worried about, but I used to give that to me mother. I used to tap dance, high kick, do splits, pull my legs up at the back of my head. I was a clever little girl. I started when I was nine and carried on till I was fifteen but I didn't turn round (spin) very good. I got so bad I couldn't do it so I gave up.

John faced a continual turnover with his juvenile troupes. His first one, *Les Jolies Petites,* disappeared after its tour of England and Tiller never used the name again. Possibly Northern audiences found the French an affectation as the original subtitle, the *Excelsiors,* was used many times.

He now formed two child duets. The *Forget-me-nots* were billed as 'the smallest song and dance act' and eventually blossomed into a team of eight, fronted by Amy Knott. The other duet was called the *Sisters Iris.* John heard Cissie Iris, the elder girl, singing a song with the principal boy from the circle during the show. Never off duty for a moment, he took her into his training school and soon gave her a booking in his spectacular, *Jack and Jill.* She progressed eventually to the title role, playing it 500 times.

Tiller waited until her younger sister was capable of putting over a song and dance, and then sent them off touring the country as a double act.

Although he preferred to train dancers from the age of nine, by the time the pantomime season came he had so many to cast he had to accept adults and teach them after they had finished a day's work. Emma Southworth went with two of her workmates to classes every evening after she finished at the mill. She remembered that John's only rehearsal place at the time was in a long room above a sundry warehouse in Lower Moseley Street. She thought 'Mr John' was very strict but kind. He had a long stick which he would place under their legs when doing the high kick to indicate where it should reach.

She spoke of tears at times until they got it right but accepted the suffering as he had no favourites and called them all his 'dolly girls'. There was no tea break but Mr John and a woman, who she thought might have been a chaperone, would go into a little room at the end, where she fancied they had a nip or two.

Tiller's theatrical enterprises were expanding so fast it became inconvenient to use his warehouse during the evenings and at weekends, so he took over part of St James's Hall in Oxford Street, Manchester, adjoining the St James's Theatre. Now that he had premises that could be used day and night, he made sure his talents and availability were known. He placed regular advertisements in a trade journal, *Music Hall,* listing the troupes and soloists that were available with references to their most prestigious bookings. In return, *Music Hall* carried photographs and

Bessie Cohen (centre) and her colleagues at a rehearsal of the Troubadour act c.1895

articles about Tiller's achievements, so spreading his fame still further. No previous dance troupe manager had attacked the entertainment world so vigorously.

Of all his soloists, Bessie Cohen had pride of place. Her sister Anne, too, was later billed as 'little Annie'. Bessie often fronted one of his most successful lines, the *Troubadours.* They consisted of six, occasionally seven, statuesque women in the style of the day. Putting his *Minnehaha Minstrels* experience to good use, Tiller trained them to play banjos and mandolins, and to sing in harmony as well as high kick. They toured the country for many years with great success.

He also taught the mandolin to four small girls and called them the *Fairy Four.* They went out to South Africa for Luscombe Searelle, an ostentatious gentleman who advertised the fact that he owned theatres in Johannesburg and Kimberley. He organized his shows with military precision, gaining the admiration of Tiller, who became his British representative.

Searelle invited artistes to contact him by first writing to John, who thus became responsible for their standards. Eight companies consisting of twelve acts were sent out at ten-week intervals, and the actual length of engagement was twelve weeks.

Settled in his large premises in Manchester, John devised a pastoral ballet called *Rustic Revelry*. It was a brilliant exercise using one hundred children, trained of course, with only a handful of principals. The entire production including scenery, props and wardrobe would be transported from town to town and then most of the children recruited locally. The show was flexible and he could slot his best troupes in and out, thus

(TILLERS) FORGET-ME-NOTS.

ensuring a regular wage for them and constantly rehearsed lines for him, all ready at a moment's notice to go to South Africa, the continent or the best halls in London.

In 1893 he extended his theatrical pursuits well beyond dance arranging when he became producer of the summer season show at the Palace Theatre, Isle of Man. All his favourite soloists appeared, many fronting his best troupes; Amy Knott with the *Forget-me-nots,* Bessie as usual with the *Troubadours* and Maggie Rimmer and the new *Rainbow* troupe who slipped off during the run to do a couple of weeks at the London Pavilion and the Oxford, then returned to complete the season.

He was also presenting ballets in a similar format to *Rustic Revelry*. He called them spectaculars and would set up the storyline, do the lyrics and librettos with J. J. Wood and co-write the music with Cuthbert Clarke. Costumes and sets were also made under his supervision. Having found a successful formula, he kept to it. Within a year he could provide eight spectaculars, all ingeniously flexible to fit one- to three-hour bookings. He kept many numbers simple enough for local children to perform (*The*

In 1893 the *Forget-me-nots* were billed as the 'smallest dancers on the variety stage'. They were vocalists as well as dancers. The boy featured is one of John's few boy artistes: Little Barnette

Grand March of the 64 Flower Gatherers was typical) and of course every show could guarantee House Full signs, with relations and friends packing the theatre every night.

Although he could be seen at rehearsals of his shows in small English towns, Tiller was an international name now. On the continent his troupes were popular in Germany and had regular bookings at the Paris Olympia and the Casino de Paris. A trio of premier dancers trained by him toured in George Edwards' Gaiety Girl companies in America and Australia.

His business enterprise knew no bounds. He set up a Christmas Carnival, taking over the entire St James's hall and theatre complex, putting on side shows and trade exhibits. He also set up a theatrical agency with a J. H. Milburn. The partnership was not a success, however, and within six months Milburn took it over and amalgamated with Nathan and Sommers.

Sarah Wood showing the elegant costumes that John provided c.1905

Whilst keeping his Manchester activities going, his most important move in the late 1890s was to take rooms at Trafalgar House, Great Newport Street, in London. Not only was it more convenient for his financial deals in international negotiations to be done there, but he needed more dancers. He had accepted so much work that he was committed to supply a hundred dancers for the pantomime season alone. He had trained all the suitable women in the Manchester area. It had been years since he could supply pupils solely trained by him. But even with his new London base it was impossible to gather enough talent from both his schools for the coming Christmas, so he advertised for dancers in the trade papers and took a chance that he could knock them into shape.

The new school was called the Tiller Training School and Lyric Academy. The move to the capital was a great upheaval for the Manchester girls, for not only did they now have to rehearse in Sin City as they called it, but they also had to work with Londoners. The two sets of girls might just have well come from two countries at war. Accents were so strong they could not even understand each other. The northerners thought the others posh and 'mardy' (affected), while in return they were found to be coarse and vulgar. There was no doubt, however, in Tiller's mind, as to which group worked harder. Until the day he died, he would praise his northern girls above all others.

All Tiller Girls loathe the description 'chorus girls': its offensiveness dates from this time. As a troupe they were paid to perform their own 'spech' (speciality number). In pantomime or musical comedy they might also be required to appear in production numbers with the rest of the company but true chorus dancers were always kept in the background. The best shows in London had girls who worked as showgirls. The difference? Dancers danced and showgirls 'showed'. The latter wafted about but certainly never danced. Men in the audience would fall in love with the beauty of these women who did little else but walk about in beautiful costumes.

Newspaper articles now called John's dancers 'Tiller's Girls'. Like Gaiety Girls they had been judged worthy of a separate identity. From now on the capital G would always be used in reference to them.

By the turn of the century, which was only ten years since his first professional engagement, John Tiller had amassed a great fortune for himself whilst changing the lives of working-class girls by giving them good wages and a career. He was to continue to revolutionize dance in the commercial theatre and become the most successful dancing master of his time.

2

Blackpool Children Get Their Chance

IN 1900 Tiller had an idea for a routine which excited him so much he could hardly wait to show it to the public. The number was extremely complicated so realising that completion would take some time, he took out advertisements a year before of the first performance and announced that bookings would be accepted for the unseen act. The *Mystic Hussars,* as it was called, proved to be so popular and successful that it was performed for over 40 years. Rival troupes gave so many imitations that its inventor was forgotten. Of all routines that ex-Tillers recall, the 'Hussars' gives the most pleasure because of the overwhelming response from the audience.

The *Mystic Hussars* routine was performed for years. Ethel Helliwell is seen checking the electric wiring which made possible the spectacular effects

As the front curtain rose, the entire stage was blacked out by drapes which also concealed twelve doors at regular intervals. All the audience saw were twelve soldiers marching slowly towards them apparently from miles away. This illusion was achieved by slightly blinding them with blue lamps facing them and lowering dummy bodies from the flies. At the point when the puppets disappeared behind the doors, there was a crash of music. Exactly at the same time the Girls, who had each been standing behind a door, burst through and on to the stage. They wore white military costumes in the style of musketeers; the fabric was impregnated with luminous paint which glowed as they marched and countermarched in the stage blackout. Then each Girl put her heels into a small square on the stage floor, connecting up with the power source. The girls were wired up so that the current lit up their cockades and enabled their swords to give off sparks as they fenced. This startling routine delighted the audience so much that they usually refused to let the show continue until an encore had been performed — often two.

Many hours of tears and frayed tempers were suffered in order to complete this intricate routine. John had a vision of what he wanted, but not being able to dance, was absolutely frustrated at times trying to get over his ideas. 'Christ almighty,' he would shout, slap his forehead, slam down his walking cane and storm out. He'd cool off while he took a walk. The Girls were not highly trained dancers and were frankly terrified of him.

In press interviews he arrogantly stated that the Italian schools of dance were too exacting, too inflexible. He claimed his pupils never came to hate their work. Certainly all reports spoke of genuine smiles on the Girls' faces, of their brightness and animation.

Elsie Parker had 'lived in' during her training. Her description is at odds with Tiller's. She maintained that you simply stood and watched the other Girls; this was called 'sitting at the side of Nellie' (Nellie or Eleanor being the only daughter John allowed to take part in the business.). Anne Liddy agrees there was no real training: 'In Tiller's you didn't learn, you just followed on. Copied it.'

It was not difficult for Anne since she had been encouraged by her father to practise her clog dancing on the kitchen hearth. Together they would go to the Tivoli and Grand Theatres in Manchester, and when they got home he would get her to imitate the dances she had seen. Anne decided to get into Tiller's troupes. She lived in Salford and was so poor that she often had to walk all the way to Manchester to rehearse. John was delighted, not only with her considerable ability but also with her smallness, and put her into the *Manchester Mites.*

The *Mites* did a great deal of touring and were given outdoor clothing, often a hooded cloak, socks and shoes, even a suitcase each. This helped the really poor to look equal to the more affluent while at the same time providing a walking advertisement for John Tiller. As a sign of their professionalism, each had her own make-up box. They were supervised by a Miss Walker who, although she could not dance, also watched over their dances and made them up every night. This was a simple job as the aim was to look younger than their years: flesh colour for the face, blue greasepaint smeared on the eyelids and a little rouge on their cheeks.

Experiences with digs, good and bad, Anne Liddy took in her stride:

We went into one place and there was a carpet on the sitting room floor, it was nicely set out. When we got back, they'd taken the carpet and some of the furniture away. Plenty of bed bugs, they would drop on top of you. You got out as quickly as you could the next morning otherwise they could get into your skin.

Often sleeping four to a bed, they made up this rhyme:

'When dancers sleep in a bed,
Four at the bottom
Four at the head,
You scratch their noses
And they tickle your toes-es.'

Anne remembers sleeping seven to a bed but at ninety-six years of age was still puzzling out where the eighth member of the troupe ended up. She would creep down the stairs in the middle of the night to raid the larder, hoping to cut a slice from one of the enormous cheeses stacked there, trusting the landlady would not notice. Her worst fright on one of these ventures was seeing what appeared to be fluorescent fish on a single stick. These turned out to be a row of haddocks.

The *Manchester Mites* were a huge success. When they worked in their home town, the audience would queue round the block to see them perform twice nightly. They were usually billed as the star attraction so John obviously made a good profit out of them but they were still paid at the same rate as all his juveniles, five shillings a week. Their pay was, however, increased when he loaned them to Madame Rasimi to work in Lyons and Bordeaux, and they were proud to be able to send almost ten shillings weekly to their mothers.

Now that he had established himself in London with a training school and offices, John decided to expand his headquarters in Manchester. He moved from St James's Hall to a large, sedate house in Lime Grove, and swiftly converted it into a combination of a commercial office, a factory and a school of physical culture. A staff of clerks dealt with correspondence, typing lyrics and dialogues and hand-copying band parts. There were small studios for authors and composers to work in.

An army of seamstresses repaired costumes and cut and sewed new ones, working in a room that resembled a large draper's shop with dozens of drawers from ceiling to floor, each crammed with accessories and shoes. The property room looked like a theatrical battlefield with masks and armour lying around in different stages of completion.

There was a gymnasium equipped with ropes, Indian clubs, parallel bars and fencing equipment. The largest area, a hall in which Tiller claimed he could train 200 pupils at any one time, was dominated by three enormous mirrors that would show the girls their mistakes. Curiously there were no barres, the rails at hip height used for ballet practice.

Though the business was thriving, there was one aspect that gave him great concern and over which he was powerless to exercise any sort of control. The Girls were so attractive that his relations were courting them and marrying the most beautiful ones behind his back. It was natural for the Girls to go out with men but Tiller was possessive and seemed to expect them to remain single until they were about thirty years of age, then quietly fade away. When one of them married he gave the impression of feeling betrayed.

His first loss was Marie Millward. She was one of his favourite leading ladies. Only two of his performers were ever allowed to place individual advertising cards in *Music Hall:* Bessie Cohen and Marie. When, of all people, his estranged cousin Sam suddenly married Marie in 1902, not only was John annoyed, but there was outrage on both sides of the highly intolerant Tiller family. Sam found himself completely cut off by his own side of the family, who considered he had married beneath him; while John had a furious row with him because he did not think Sam good enough for Marie.

The couple had a daughter, Marjorie, who grew up deprived of contact with paternal relatives and excluded from any news of John and his work. The little girl persuaded her mother to share some of her memories of her dancing life, though in secret from Sam: and it was not long before Marjorie inevitably developed an ambition to become a Tiller Girl herself.

The beautiful Elizabeth Tomkins who worked for John for seven years before marrying his second son, Robert

Then John's second son, Robert, married the stunningly beautiful Elizabeth Tomkins who had been dancing for seven years. Robert had never been a healthy man and found it difficult to earn a living. As his family began to grow, money was hard to come by so he became a clerk for his family and John cannily gave dressmaking work to his new daughter-in-law to help them survive whilst getting good value for money for himself. Just as she had been a conscientious dancer, she now became an equally conscientious needlewoman. Elizabeth toiled for hours on end and her children remember her machine going non-stop. Great wicker baskets were trundled in and out of their home but she never complained nor spoke of regretting the end of her dancing life.

The Tiller fame and fortune had also become an attraction for hangers-on to members of his family. Nellie, the eldest child and closest to John, married an aspiring theatrical agent and manager, Percy Rimmer. He was immediately dubbed a ne'er-do-well and a bad lot by the family, and the Girls quickly learnt to get out of his reach whenever he was around. They had to meet up with Nellie a great deal as she was supervising the school's wardrobe. If they mentioned him, she would mutter, 'Don't talk to me about that rat.' This confused the Girls' uncomplicated minds as they knew the couple were still living together. Eventually Nellie got rid of Percy Rimmer and replaced him with Robert Clarke, who did Tiller's stage effects. Dumpy, down-to-earth Nellie faced facts and realised people would spot the difference in age between herself and Robert, so decided to confuse them all by calling him her adopted son. He, at least, kept his hands off the Girls but he did flirt with Nellie's young nieces whom he would take out on the quiet.

John's wife Mary and daughters

To add to John's uneasiness at seeing his Girls and family mingling to his loss, there was deep concern about his wife. For many months a nurse had been taking care of Mary, described by everyone as a gentle, retiring person. She was seriously ill with cancer of the womb. She had never been involved in his business and as it grew, saw considerably less of her husband. Now she was literally wasting away, and his visits were still infrequent. Her unmarried daughters Florence, Bertha and Jessie, however, lived at home and gave her what comfort they could.

Mary died in February, 1905, aged fifty. Only twenty months later, John married his second wife Jennie. His children appeared to feel no bitterness about her stepping so swiftly into their mother's shoes. She never attempted to take Mary's place, but simply extended her considerable warmth and kindness to them.

There is no doubt that Jennie Walker had played quite a part in John's life before they were married. She had been given a programme credit for making dresses several years before. She had been supervising classes at the Manchester school and was, in fact, the Miss Walker that Anne Liddy remembered making her up on tour. It is highly likely that she was the same woman that Emma Southwick imagined was having a nip with Tiller in the back room during rehearsals way back in the St James's Hall times.

From the start Jennie was surrounded by gossip. It was rumoured she had been a barmaid, heady stuff in those days. The combination of the sophisticated impresario with his driving ambition and the outspoken Newcastle woman with her earthy language and manner to match, made them appear a strange couple. John, of course, had long since lost his northern accent and took delight in his appearance as the well-heeled businessman. Whatever their difference on the surface, their union was excellent for business. She was to remain childless and showered all her love on every single Girl at the school.

She scoured the streets in the poorer areas looking for likely candidates and then, knowing the reality of poverty, taught them the rules of hygiene in her own way, which the Girls would imitate and laugh at behind her back. 'You have a bath and powder well in between,' she would say, oblivious of their embarrassment. She would give money to them to have their hair done. 'Go and get your hair crimped and tinted.' The canny ones would simply have their hair set and buy a good meal with the remainder. She would never notice that the hair had not been done.

Jennie was already a dynamic force in John's business by the time they were married and almost to celebrate it, when he had a publicity brochure printed with engraved illustrations of the dancers, pride of place went to portraits of himself and his bride.

There always had been ambivalent feelings between father and oldest son. At the wedding ceremony, when the usual problem of naming his father had arisen, John put 'Lawrence Tiller (deceased)' but his son was called Lawrence, was still alive and now a man of twenty-nine, working as general manager in the business. His flirtatious manner was a cause of great concern to John; he had lost too many dancers to marriage with his own relations, but had reckoned without his secretary, Amy Bradley. She had set her sights on Lawrence and married him within a year of John's own ceremony.

At Easter in 1900 John Tiller produced his first show at the Winter Gardens Pavilion, Blackpool. The *Tiller Quartette* appeared in *Jack Ashore*; it was described as a 'Patriotic Spectacle' and set in 1805 in a village in Cornwall. By the summer, the same show had been enlarged and retitled *Jolly Jack* or *The Heart that Beats for a Sailor*. The programme claimed that there were 100 artistes in the cast. Admission was sixpence and the elegance of the audience was mirrored in a programme note: 'Ladies of the Pavilion Stalls are kindly requested to remove their hats'. This was the time when hats resembled wedding cakes with layers of chiffon, tulle, feathers and even birds.

Elizabeth Tomkins in the lead role in 'Jolly Jack' c.1901

This production in 1900 started a long association with Blackpool. John quickly became intimate friends with Mr Huddlestone, the general manager of the Winter Gardens complex, and together they produced more scenes and numbers during the summer season and well into the autumn. The shows that year were such a success with holidaymakers and residents that they continued to produce entertainment there for twenty-five years. Tiller was allowed complete freedom of ideas, an opportunity he readily grasped. Excited by the countries he saw on his travels, he wanted to share his impressions with the audiences and did so in scenarios such as *From Monte Carlo to Japan*. His fondness for rustic scenes inspired *The Quaint Old Village of Honeysuckle Hollow*. One year he produced a comic sketch called *The Magic Hotel or How Tommy and his Uncle Herbert Spent a Quiet Night*.

BLACKPOOL CHILDREN GET THEIR CHANCE

Usually the spring show was a rehash of the summer show from the previous year. Repeating numbers would quickly get the artistes in trim and once the show was on they would start rehearsing for the main summer production and perform at the same time. A patriotic number was always featured. Tiller usually co-wrote the music, always visualized the scenic designs, executed them and also supplied the stage properties, charging the Winter Gardens management for all services. It was the same moneymaking format as his touring spectaculars. After the season the show would tour the country with a few troupes from the original cast and local children appearing in the large scenes.

Local children were very keen to get work for the long season at Blackpool. There was a rival organization at the Tower Ballroom headed by Madame Pauline Rivers who had established a good reputation years before Tiller arrived. Young though they were, her pupils knew she could not provide the amount of professional work that he had to offer. Little Ethel Helliwell heard about John's auditions while in the middle of a rehearsal for the Tower show:

Although I was only nine, I was determined to get in. I pretended to see a pin on the floor. I kept pretending to pick it up and others, getting further and further to the door picking them up. When I got there, I ran like mad.

A troupe at Blackpool c.1900

Ethel ran out of the door with the frightening single-mindedness that later made her the most successful Tiller Girl. She was eventually in charge of 160 dancers at one point, and she choreographed productions all over the world. She commuted by air between England, France and Monte Carlo, took a Hollywood screen test, only to turn her back on America for her love of a famous impresario. But her career started simply playing a sailor on a battleship, in the background of her first show.

One of John's earliest troupes, the Superba Quartette

So the little Blackpool girls got their first taste of the world of entertainment. They would be placed into various troupes: the *Merry Mascots,* the *Snowdrops* or the *Twelve Twinkling Stars,* in accordance with their heights and talents. The biggest attraction, the *Manchester Mites,* came to Blackpool to work the season with them. This created a few problems as intense rivalry was felt between the children from the two towns. 'Blackpool used to be a riot when we walked out,' said one Mite. They would be marshalled back to their digs, proudly wearing their uniforms. Remarks were made by the local rivals, not about dancing standards as the *Mites* were inevitably highly experienced and could not be faulted, but more was made of their apparent roughness:

> Mr Tiller got these Girls from Manchester, they were the lowest of the low. That was in the beginning. Then he started getting Girls from Blackpool, they were a better class. He got better Girls from there, not boasting.

This attitude is still held by many early Tillers today. Dolly Ashby auditioned when she was eleven years old. She had a confusing family background, as many children did in those days. As her natural mother had been unable to care for her, she had been taken in and looked after by an uncle and aunt. She was so happy with them, she called them Dad and Mum and living only a few streets away from her real mother, would visit her daily, calling her 'My mother's sister'.

She was accepted for the Winter Gardens show, immediately struck up a great friendship with Edith Whalley and they became inseparable. When Tiller offered her work abroad, she refused, being frightened to travel too far away from home.

Whole families of female relations worked for Tiller. Nepotism was rife. 'Have you got any more girls?' Jennie would ask the mothers. The Helliwell family not only supplied Ethel of the Iron Will but her twin sister Alice, and elder sisters Elsie and Mabel. All four Girls eventually danced all over the world, sending quite a considerable amount of money home to their mother.

Edith Whalley had an older sister Gertie. They had been orphaned and were so desperate for work that they auditioned while still mourning.

> Black dresses right down to our ankles. We had an older sister at home. She had to go to work too. I can't remember the wages they paid us but we couldn't get work in the shops anyway.

The two sisters bravely tried to support their family home with their salaries. One day they took their niece, Doris Carter, to a rehearsal:

> I was only just eight. Mrs Tiller said 'Go on, get into the line.' They pushed me in. I said, 'I haven't come for that.' They took no notice. I told them I wasn't old enough but Mrs Tiller said I was tall enough and she would work it. My mother had a fit when I went home and my aunt said I'd been taken on.

Once the show opened at the Winter Gardens, Tiller would disappear on his travels round the world. Jennie preferred to stay and supervise; she was always backstage seeing to their make-up:

> There used to be a mile-long queue to be made up. All God's fear on earth used to be behind Mrs Tiller. We never wanted to be the first one when she had a new stick of make-up as she didn't take the cellophane wrapper off. It used to scratch your face. We daren't tell her, we were so frightened of her. We would push each other to the front of the

queue. You'd have to be in your vest. My mother had time on her hands so made my underwear. She looked down and said, 'Who's made your knickers?' I went scarlet at the word 'knickers'.

Edith Whalley, looking like a modern day punk, who auditioned in strict mourning dress

Aged 11, and already showing her strength of character, Billie Bart in the Bristol pantomime 'Dick Whittington', 1900. She was to become the sort of opportunist that John would have admired: her second marriage was bigamous and when she was in her sixties she returned to Britain from America in order to marry a consultant surgeon at Bart's Hospital. Unfortunately he slipped from her grasp by dying

An example of the ornate
costumes that John designed

With the Winter Gardens show employing 100 to 300 artists every
summer and the schools in London and Manchester training others all the
year round, there was a never-ending pool of dancers instructed in the
Tiller style. Both Mr and Mrs Tiller were always on the lookout for any
child or woman with potential. In 1906, a seventeen-year-old orphan
called Jane Balfe was working in a factory. Her friend Angela, who
worked for Tiller every year in pantomime, asked Jane to accompany her

35

to the stage door of the Hippodrome Theatre, Manchester, to pick up a contract. Jane describes the incident:

> Whilst Angela was signing the contract, John Tiller himself walked in. He said, 'Hello Angela, are you coming back to work with us again?' He then turned to me and asked if I was signing a contract too. I replied that I couldn't dance. He said, 'That doesn't matter. I'll show you what we want. Let me see your teeth.' Apparently he always reckoned a pretty girl with a lovely smile was more important than any other quality; so the teeth had to be good. He then asked to see my legs. I was terribly embarrassed; not only was I a convent girl but the skirts were worn down to the ankles and women just didn't show their legs in those days. Angela told me not to worry; Mr Tiller was used to seeing girls' legs. I pulled my skirt up a little but he said he'd have to see higher than that to make sure my legs weren't bowed at the knees so I did as I was told.

Jane agreed to go into pantomime. The work was fairly easy — just a little movement, not the high kicking style of the true Tiller line. She was overjoyed to find she earned a much higher wage than for her factory work. This was important to her as she was self-supporting and had found it tough going in the last two years. Relatives had taken on the boys of her family but did not want the responsibility and lower wages of the girls. She had had to rough it alone in digs since she was fifteen.

In the last week of the pantomime, Jennie asked her if she would like to learn to dance properly, adding that Mr Tiller didn't like girls already trained but preferred them to learn his way. Knowing she had to support herself, they paid her while she trained at the Manchester school. She had to provide her practice outfit which consisted of a short skirt of any colour, just above knee length, with a blouse. They continued to pay her while rehearsing and with seven other Girls, she was sent on tour round England.

The stage costumes were ornate, the hemline above the knee and worn with knickers massed with frills so that no outline of the leg could be seen. That would have been considered vulgar. Often the skirt was frilled as well making it impossible for the audience to see where the skirt ended and the knickers began. Tights, which Jane had to pay for herself, were made of thickish cotton and fastened with a coin each side and taped. They rarely showed their hair on stage as enormous head-dresses or wigs were worn.

As well as her tights, Jane had to bear the cost of tipping the callboy and dresser every week. The other Girls would have had to send money home but Jane set aside a similar sum to tide her over periods of unemployment. The morning rehearsals each day were a Tiller rule not demanded by the management and so were not paid for. In these sessions they practised their kicking and wheeling; John brought in a sergeant-major to train them in military marching. The quick turn of the head, called dressing in army terms, was to check that the line was dead straight, and woe betide them if it wasn't.

Although there was always precision team work, they also had solo

spots within the number, called 'individuals' by the Girls. A reporter at the time describes the *La Scala Girls* at the Palace:

They make their appearance in charming costumes of pale blue and each one a replica, to the minutist detail of the other seven. They sing a buoyant chorus song and march around the stage whilst performing evolutions. Eventually they make an exit in a long rectangular line, all with arms extended. Then follow several individual performances. One member of the troupe submits a graceful skipping rope dance and another with a tambourine gives an exhibition of her skill as an acrobatic dancer.

Afterwards the whole party take the stage again and the orchestra strikes up a seductive 'coon' melody. The Girls commence a tuneful lilting chorus and subsequently go through the familiar 'cakewalk' evolutions. They do them though, with a wonderful spirit and grace and two of them present a kind of duet which evokes a spontaneous roar of applause. A particular feature of their performance is the marvellous precision and clockwork-like regularity of action they maintain, even in the most intricate figures. The effect of the whirling figures all moving identically is curious and fascinating.

37

Literally queueing round the block for a Tiller show, 'Monte Carlo to Tokio' at the Winter Gardens, Blackpool, in 1902

Jane had to master the eye make-up of the day. It was quite an art. Called 'hot black', it consisted of a stick of black greasepaint of which a small spoonful was held over a lit candle; when it was melted, blobs of the hot grease would be put on each eyelash with a hairpin. Gradually it dried and more would be added until the eyelashes were laden. John's obsession for uniformity was thwarted at this point as the experience of the older Girls always showed in their eye make-up. Their lashes would be heavily caked whereas the newcomers were fearful of the technique at first.

The face make-up was known as 'fleshing'; it was then a natural colour, not the tan that became popular later on. The white dusting powder over the fleshing was sometimes cornflour. Every evening the make-up would be wiped off with a towel resulting in quite a large laundry bill for each Girl. The biggest crime of all was to go round to the front of house or into the street in 'full slap', as stage make-up was called.

Life was hell for unsuccessful acts; not only did the performers have to put up with heckling and catcalls but they had to be agile enough to duck the rotten eggs and fruit thrown by a disgruntled audience. The fact that they had brought these missiles with them showed their aggressive intentions. Many artistes got drunk before they faced the ordeal on stage. If a couple of drinks helped to steel the nerves, a full bottle made it thoroughly bearable.

Every night the show finished at eleven; after the Saturday performance they would have to pack the stage costumes and props carefully into skips which were large wicker baskets which could be thrown around without harm to the contents. Then they would all go for a fish and chip supper. They had to be up early on Sunday morning to get to the station to travel to the next venue which was inevitably the other side of the country.

Being a shy person, Jane was often overawed by the landladies. One woman was so mean that she turned out all the lights immediately they got into their bedroom. She had not told them the whereabouts of the lavatory. Halfway through the night, they decided they needed to know, went out on to the landing, groped around but in desperation had to go back to their room, pee in their shoes and empty them out of the window!

However, Jane loved dancing and the new life that was opening up for her, but when she was offered work in 1907 at the English Theatre, Paris, she was frankly scared. Rumours abounded of white slave traffic. Newspaper stories told how innocent women strolling the streets of foreign countries would ignore the feeling of a slight pin prick in the arm and next minute would find themselves in brothels. Immediately she saw Paris, she forgot any anxiety. She fell in love with the elegant shops, the boulevards lined with trees, the outdoor cafés, especially the small one next to the theatre where the Girls congregated before the show.

Once it was known the dancers frequented the café, the Stage Door Johnnies started gathering. Always courteous, they would first announce their presence by sending messages or flowers. One particularly persistent suitor sent Jane postcards every day. Unknown to her, he would be in the café while she ate. As it was rumoured amongst the Girls that horsemeat was served, she was unadventurous and always stuck to a monotonous diet of egg and chips. When she came to pay for the bill, she found that it had already been paid. This frequently happened and the waiter refused to

Looking unusually demure,
Jennie Walker who became
the second Mrs Tiller

tell her which man it was. When he eventually introduced himself, she politely told him that she would rather pay her own bill and had enough money to do so.

By now, some of Tiller's Girls were truly world travellers; the best troupes had bookings in Paris, St Petersburg, San Francisco, Berlin, Cape Town, Hanover, Geneva, Vienna, Buenos Aires and Hamburg. Their journeys were well organized by the super-efficient Head Girls but of course occasionally plans went awry. The Palace Girls had an unfortunate experience trying to reach Paris. It was arranged that they should get the express train from Hanover in order to open at the Folies-Bergère on the very evening of their arrival. To their dismay, they arrived at the departure platform just in time to see the express pulling out. As it was imperative that they get to Paris as quickly as possible they embarked on a slow train, hoping to arrive in time for their turn at the theatre. What they did not realize was that the express train had a restaurant car and the slow train did not. The Palace Girls, needless to say, were hungry to start with; nevertheless they had to exist for seventeen long hours on bananas and chocolate picked up at wayside stations. When they eventually got to Paris, they found that they might just as well have stopped and had a meal in Hanover. The opening night of the Folies had been postponed for two days. What did they do next? They simply made a raid on the first restaurant they came to and gave the proprietor fits.

Nudity was now presented on stage and one producer tried to coax Jane into leaving Tiller for this work. She was appalled when he explained to her she would be required to pose in a picture frame. It would not be true nudity, he assured her; she would wear a body stocking. She would only have to sit still and clever stage lighting would make it appear as though she were naked. Jane had no hesitation in refusing although she had no work offered after that particular season. She always felt sad at the end of the run. The other Girls would talk about their families and homes which made her feel so lonely.

It was a contradiction that although John was warm to his Girls he was emotionally quite remote from his own children. Yet he had always generously supported his mother and half-brother. When he offered to buy her a house in Blackpool, her request was for a simple terrace house, similar to the one in which they had spent their early life together. She settled in Crocker Street and he visited her regularly during rehearsals of the Winter Gardens shows. After a short illness in 1909 she died. Now the declaration of her age on the death certificate was out of her control, the truth was listed at last. She was seventy-eight.

His mother had been a pragmatic woman, always making the best of the most difficult situations, earning a livelihood as a needlewoman to help her sons when young and later during John's early theatrical ventures. She had lived to see him prove himself beyond all her expectations. As his fame and fortune grew, she never became ostentatious and refused all his efforts to encourage her into a more luxurious life.

Like all successful businessmen, John was willing to delegate responsibility to a trusted circle of people while he developed new contacts. In Manchester his new wife and eldest daughter were in charge of the school in Lime Grove, the theatrical stores and the annual Winter Gardens show in Blackpool. He put Madame Sismondi, whom he had booked years before to go to South Africa, in charge of his London school. When her act split up, he offered her a permanent studio within the premises where she could run her own classes. In return she supervised the classical side of his training school.

He was making a small fortune with his spectacular ballets which toured the whole year round. Always involved with every side of the production and never one to hide his light under a bushel, he was credited in every programme as co-writing, composing, designing, and making props and scenery — a one-man band. He dominated his many touring pantomimes too. In order to store the increased amount of scenery and wardrobe, he bought new premises at Heald Grove, Rusholme, and his daughter Nellie was put in charge.

John failed dismally, however, when he set up any business with a partner. He was so autocratic that he had to dominate every enterprise. Just as his earlier attempt to form a theatrical agency ended in failure within six months, a later venture with George Sheldon failed in 1902 with equally bad feelings. Then there was the abrupt dismissal of his German representative through the columns of *Music Hall*: 'Herr Obermeyer no longer has any connection with these Schools.' John subsequently opened a training establishment with Will Bishop, a famous performer, which they called the 'Hygienic School of Dancing'. Again this swiftly closed. No one, it seemed, could work on equal terms with him. He was so forceful and dogmatic in his ideas that the Girls would be embarrassed at band calls when he interrupted acts, totally unknown to him, to tell them what he thought was wrong.

At the turn of the century, he had been excited by his conception of the *Mystic Hussars* routine. Now ten years later he conceived a simple notion: as the Girls were kicking, he got them to link their arms around each other's waists. Proximity would help them work well together. At last it was possible for them to achieve absolute precision. His dream had come true. He would have been proud to know that this was the idea that really made his name for posterity. Even in the 1980s a troupe could be performing a highly individual routine in the most modern style but they only had to link arms, synchronize a few kicks and the audience would break into spontaneous applause. Whatever fame future choreographers were to have in the commercial theatre, not one could claim such an instantaneous reaction.

The highly popular 'Tally Ho' that is still copied in pantomimes today

3

How John Retrieves a Lost Fortune,
But Loses a Son

THROUGHOUT his theatrical career, Tiller produced hundreds of troupes, giving them names like the *Snowdrops,* the *Four Champions,* the *Imperial Quartette,* and so on. Each line had its speciality; it might comprise exceptionally small girls, or very tall ones, or talented acrobats, but whatever the speciality, all could sing and dance. There is no doubt that the standard in his troupes was excellent; his pride in his reputation would not allow public appearances unless all the routines were impeccable. Occasionally the chemistry within the troupe resulted in exceptional work and it would become his crack troupe.

The Palace Girls were one such top line team. Before they were formed for regular bookings at the Palace Theatre, London, every Girl had considerable experience in dancing. The line became instantly popular and managements all over the world were impatient to snap them up whenever they were free. Whilst resident at the Palace, their conductor was Herman Finck, a composer who collaborated with John for the Winter Gardens seasons. He admired Tiller, describing him as a genius at organizing and directing his Girls but also noting that John ordered everyone about in a dictatorial way. This was hilarious as Finck himself was equally autocratic.

One evening Finck proclaimed that a piece of music that Tiller had composed for a skipping-rope routine was dull and lifeless and that neither he nor the Girls could do a thing with it. He remembered a piece of music he had been carrying around in his head for years and bragged that he knew a better tune. 'If you can do your dance tonight without a band rehearsal, I'll play a lovely melody.' He was arrogant enough to expect them to dance to music they had never heard. The Girls knew that their reputation for dancing as one was at stake, but because they were so well drilled and were accustomed to Finck's ways, it worked brilliantly.

In 1912 the Palace Girls were selected to represent all Tiller Girls when they were greatly honoured by being invited to perform at the very first Royal Command Performance. Although troupes of Tiller's dancers eventually appeared in more than twenty-four such shows, it was to mean more than any other Royal Command in that the acts were personally chosen by the King and Queen. They had regularly appeared before the rich and famous but this audience included a dazzling array of royalty: the King and Queen, the Grand Duchess George of Russia, Princess Victoria, the Princesses Christiana and Victoria of Schleswig-Holstein, Prince Arthur of Connaught, the Duke and Duchess of Teck, Prince Alexander of Teck, and Princess Henry of Battenberg.

HOW JOHN RETRIEVES A LOST FORTUNE, BUT LOSES A SON

The front of the Palace Theatre was presented as a flower garden with the Royal Box transformed with a bower of roses. The Girls had the third spot in the first half of a bill shared with George Robey, Harry Lauder, Little Titch and Anna Pavlova. The souvenir programme, looking like an enormous chocolate box covered in purple velvet, included a photograph of John Tiller with eight portraits of the Girls round him. Their act was called *A Fantasy in Black and White*. For their routine they wore white curled wigs beneath black velvet hats and white satin dresses with narrow black-edged flounces. They performed against a backdrop resembling a pen and ink drawing on white paper. It was a thoroughly tested number as Tiller had not only shown it at the Palace but his *La Scala* Girls had also performed it at the Winter Gardens Pavilion, Blackpool, the previous year. The Girls were also included in the finale which consisted of the 150 music hall artistes presenting *Variety's Garden Party*.

The Palace Girls, 1912

Managing Director: ALFRED BUTT.

The Palace Theatre

Shaftesbury Avenue.

THE PALACE GIRLS in "FRESH AIRS and GRACES"

43

Edgar Wallace, a great fan of this troupe, took a fancy to one Girl in particular and would take the whole team to the races in order to meet her. Declaring that she was so beautiful that she ought to be in pictures, he gave her some of his manuscripts. Unfortunately for him, his feelings were not reciprocated and she went off to work in America. Sydney Baynes was another admirer and he dedicated his *Destiny* waltz to them.

Always willing to undertake a new challenge, Tiller sent out a complete production to South Africa in 1912. Jane, the orphan girl, was chosen to go. All the Girls were excited but some of their parents were absolutely terrified. 'You can't go there,' said one mother, 'there are lions and tigers.' 'Not down the streets mother,' replied her knowing daughter. The journey took six weeks. Tiller travelled with them, but first class while they were relegated to steerage. Rehearsals went on as usual every morning but in order to disturb the other passengers as little as possible, they had to get up very early and work in a screened-off area.

Once in South Africa, they went to Johannesburg where they stayed for twenty weeks before going on to Durban, Port Elizabeth, Cape Town and Kimberley. They were wined and dined as never before. Many Girls became engaged, one to a Lord. The tour lasted eighteen months only, the combination of the Russian Revolution and World War I stopping the show from being a longer success. The people backing it 'bunkered' (disappeared with the money) and as Producer Tiller felt morally bound to pay off all the artistes himself as well as to find their return fares. This practically ruined him but rather than take the easy way out and declare himself bankrupt, he called a meeting of his creditors and asked for time to pay. He was too proud of his name and reputation to have the slur of bankruptcy against it. So at sixty, he started to build up his business again.

However, even when in debt, he continued to enjoy an extravagant lifestyle. He declared that his large diamond rings were his investment; they probably were as after his 'crash' some disappeared but he still maintained his two houses. Mrs Tiller presided over the one in Blackpool while he was at the grander one in Addlestone, Surrey, to which, when the Girls were playing in London, he would invite small groups for a short weekend. They were captivated by the beautiful village, played croquet on the lawn and altogether had a delightful time. Then on Monday the chauffeur drove them straight to the theatre for the show. The London headquarters now moved to stylish new premises at 143, Charing Cross Road. Not only was the rehearsal space larger but here Tiller was able to have an imposing office which he decorated with caricature drawings of himself showing large heads on small (but fat) bodies, and always with his hands clasped behind his back. There were several large photographs and the one that he was particularly fond of certainly gives the impression of the successful impresario. He favoured less one that had been taken ten years before in which his bowler hat and suit are typical of a provincial businessman.

With his attention diverted to the new studio, the honour of the Royal Command Performance and the crisis with his South African production, it is not surprising that Tiller was unaware that he was losing control of his Manchester school. As General Manager, his son Lawrence felt more able than his father would acknowledge and started his own troupes. He was so

John Tiller looking like the
typical provincial businessman

cunning about it that his dancers thought they were still working for John!
There was a showdown and in 1914 the relationship that had always been
so ambivalent was destroyed. Lawrence was thirty-six years old, the same
age at which his father had begun his own theatrical career. He was
intelligent enough to realize that his father would never allow him much
freedom in the business and so he started his own training centre at Heald
Grove, Rusholme. Amy, his wife, naturally relinquished her job as
secretary to John and actively encouraged him. Many suspected that the
move had originally been her idea. Despite the fact that he had always
called himself Lawrence, he advertised his business as the John Lawrence
School of Dancing, neatly acquiring the kudos of his father's name.

Lawrence Tiller and his wife
Amy who went into successful
competition with his own
father. Even the naïve dancers
suspected it was Amy's idea

John's pupils continued to train at Lime Grove. The road itself had become a colony of residents specializing in theatrical and allied activities. Caroline Moore, who described herself as a professor of dance, occupied number 1. Nellie Tiller lived at number 10. John, of course, was still at number 15. A school of masseurs had set up at number 17 and a rival dance director called Sherman Fisher was working from number 18. He was successful with his dance troupes for many years despite the fact that young girls did not like working for him as he was notorious for his wandering hands and slimy advances. They retaliated by cruelly nicknaming him 'the Chinese Jew'.

The three youngest of Tiller's own children married at this time. Bertha, who had been a student at art college in Manchester, wed Percy Gaunt and went with him to Shanghai. Jessie was John's youngest and sweetest child. After her mother died she went on many trips abroad with him. She was always impressed by his fame and would have liked a theatrical career. She did appear in amateur shows just as he had, but he would not allow any of his children to become professional performers. So Jessie became a secretary to a Manchester solicitor and eventually fell in love with and married an officer during the First World War. Although he showed particular fondness for Jessie, John certainly was not generous to the couple when after the war her husband wanted to set up in the textile business in Newcastle. It was *his* parents rather than John that helped them financially.

Walter, the youngest boy, had the most distant relationship with his father; he and Robert had been sent to boarding school and had seen even less of John than their sisters. When he was quite young he emigrated to Australia; his girlfriend followed and they eventually married.

It was ironic that such a prolific man should have so few grandchildren. Only Nellie, Robert and Jessie had offspring. Lawrence was the one who never seemed part of the warm family atmosphere created by his brothers and sisters. The rest of them felt his wife tried to sever all connections. She had a definite dislike for Robert's wife, the former dancer, and refused to see her as she grew older.

John Tiller and his surviving children at Bertha's wedding in 1912: kneeling l to r — Nellie, Jessie and Florence; extreme left — John Lawrence; John — next to the bride; top left — Robert; tallest on the right — Walter

John's youngest daughter
Jessie appearing in an
amateur theatrical show —
just as he had

John adored being with his grandchildren. As with his own children, he actively discouraged any of them from becoming performers. One youngster who loved to recite to him felt utterly rejected when she heard him remark that 'some unsuccessful applicants were no better than this child'. But he gave much of his time to them and showered them with expensive gifts.

Tiller began to provide entertainment in the intervals at the Empress Ballroom, Blackpool. Most of the productions shown here were patriotic spectacles requiring little dancing ability. This was an absolute godsend to beginners. A rumour that he was casting 100 children went round St James's School in Church Street, so instead of going straight home the girl pupils nipped off to the audition. Not only did half the school turn up but seemingly so did hundreds from all the schools in Blackpool. John had not expected such an overwhelming response, and as not even the Ballroom itself could contain such large numbers, he took them all outside into the street to make his selection.

Gertie Sohl, one of the lucky
schoolchildren chosen to
appear at Blackpool

Children with previous experience not only did the shows at the Pavilion
at 2 pm and 7 pm but they also appeared at the Ballroom in between,
thoroughly enjoying the mad rush. The children's troupes were graded
from tallest to smallest in order to emphasize the difference in height, the
littlest usually getting most of the laughs and applause.

Although Tiller still produced the Winter Gardens show every year, he
delegated more and more of the work there to his assistant directors as he
was so busy abroad. Once the show had had its opening night, Jennie took
over. She was there every single night, a formidable figure in her long,
black skirt, cardigan and black straw hat. The stage hands thought she
looked like a vulture waiting to pounce and would mutter that the old girl
was on the sidelines again. It was her single-mindedness in keeping the
show perfect that resulted in some very blunt speaking which some found
hard to take.

Throughout the routine she would direct the dancers. Hissing nonstop, 'Ssst, ssst. You there, number five. What do you think you're doing? You wait till you come off.' Number five became so terrified she made more mistakes and prayed to God that the dance would never finish. One unfortunate Girl had a more ample bosom than her colleagues and as Jennie could see her sticking out in front, she was ordered to get further back. Of course in doing so, her rear became out of line, so she was cussed for that too. Most of the Girls were embarrassed by her constant hissing. Others, probably because they were novices, felt it supportive. Despite her criticism of their dancing they knew she cared for them and always stepped in in any family crisis:

> She was so kind when I was orphaned, she always made sure I was fed by organizing a rota of other Girls' mothers who took me in until I was fourteen; otherwise I would have ended up in an orphanage.

Despite the fact that the Ballroom shows had comparatively short runs, every production was spectacular. One Girl reported:

A juvenile troupe, 1917

John and Jennie walking to a rehearsal at the Winter Gardens, Blackpool. The stage-hands called her a vulture, partly because of her habit of dressing in all black, but also because of her attitude

We were in the show *King and Country* and had never done anything on stage before. It was when the war was on. I was a little scout. I had a tent near the band. The others all dragged on planks and sandbags. Then we had Lights Out and when the bugle went again, the firing started. There was terrific gunfire played on the great organ. You'd have thought that the enormous Ballroom was on fire. The bugle sounded again. One soldier fell. Another was writing a letter. There was one with a stretcher and Red Cross nurses were represented. They all sang *O God our Help in Ages Past*. There wasn't a dry eye in the house.

John's crack juvenile troupe was still the *Manchester Mites* and their feuds with the local Girls still raged every spring when they emigrated to Blackpool to perform there. Their matron Daisy had a very interesting background. Unknown to them, she had been one of Tiller's favourite leading ladies around 1906, but when the work offers stopped she faced the same bleak future confronting all dancers who feel too old to dance. She was unmarried, had no relation able to support her financially and no training for any other job. She was an excellent choice to supervise the *Mites,* knowing just what tricks they could get up to. Thus she played a part in the *Mites'* continuing popularity and remained in the theatre world that she loved.

She certainly needed all her expertise one night when the children made their entrance for a skipping rope routine. They were supposed to enter just as the large velvet curtains with enormous gold tassels rose. The leading child came on slightly earlier than usual, caught her rope on one of the tassels and found herself going up. She was very frightened and had no idea what to do until Daisy managed to shout above the laughter in the audience to let go.

Like all juvenile troupes they had to go to court every Monday in a new town to obtain a licence to work. This was a means of seeing whether they looked well and that there was proper control of their curfew. Quite often police were at the stage door making sure they were out of the theatre at the regulation time. At school the other children treated them like royalty. On one occasion they got so swollen headed that they were charging the children a penny each to try on their hats. Daisy soon put a stop to that. Their education certainly suffered as the teachers did not like them interrupting the curriculum and sat them at the back of the class and told them to write home.

Although some of the *Mites* were as old as fifteen, because they were called *Mites,* their routines were always childlike. With tambourines they would sing, 'She's a ragpicker, she's a ragpicker. All the livelong day' and kick as high as they could. In another number, dressed in nightdresses and carrying candlesticks, they would sing:

> ''Tis the shadow on the wall
> Close your eyes and you won't see it at all
> Look it dances all the night
> By the moonbeams' mystic light
> 'Tis the shadow on the wall.'

The *Mites* over school age resented being with kids all the time and tried to assert their freedom. On a trip to Dublin two of them asked and received permission to share a double room away from 'the children'. Temptation proved too strong one night when there were some naval cadets in the audience who threw flowers and chocolates up to the troupe and were waiting at the stage door after the show. Somehow the Girls gave Daisy the slip and went off with them. Daisy, of course, found out and that was the end of their independence. The landladies found the *Mites* well behaved; they all had separate tasks for the day, two doing the food shopping for the troupe which the landlady would cook. Others made beds, swept and cleaned.

The Girls smoked despite the fact that it usually meant instant dismissal if they were found out. When they heard John or Jennie coming towards their dressing-rooms they would hastily open any windows and try to wave the smoke out. One Girl was caught but was too useful as a Head Girl to get the sack:

At this time we used to rehearse in long cardigans. We'd been practising hard and were having a rest, just standing around and the Head Girl

52

was smoking. Suddenly she said, 'My God, it's the Old Man', pinched out her cigarette and put it into her cardigan pocket. For a while she talked to Mr Tiller. Suddenly she realized she hadn't put it out properly and said, 'Excuse me, Mr Tiller, I think I'm on fire.'

The war presented many one-off jobs for the older Girls, usually unpaid, as they were entertaining the troops. They had to be prepared to perform in the strangest conditions. Six of them did a routine on top of a tank, and did not stop even when the snow began to fall. The most luxurious setting was a specially prepared Music Hall aboard ship. It was given at the launching of what was Britain's largest liner at the time, the S.S. *Aquitania*. The *Sunshine Tillers* appeared with George Robey and Vesta Tilley. The war also gave a chance to married dancers. Until this time, Tiller never knowingly employed them. Even if there was a booking in a Girl's home town, John's régime was so demanding that a husband would no doubt have objected to his wife giving priority to her work. But while the men were away at war, the rule was relaxed.

In order to pay his debts and restore his reputation, John took almost every job that was offered. This led him to accept work in productions that really weren't up to his standard and the increased bookings resulted in a massive turnover of dancers. It was possible for a poor girl with talent to rise through the Tiller hierarchy. The very best Halls in London were booking the Girls and there were exciting prospects of travelling abroad to all the major capitals. If a dancer showed some individuality, she was fortunate as John was still offering principal work. He had numerous bookings on the Broadhead circuit, aptly named the 'bread and butter tour' by the Girls. When he presented a complete pantomime, which naturally he had devised, directed, co-composed and co-designed, he could offer a weekly wage for an average of seventy-five artistes in each show.

Perhaps because John was fostering each Girl's personality within their 'spots' in troupe dances, this period produced the brightest Tiller sparks. The outrageous philandering May Sharples, Ethel and Mabel Helliwell who both eventually took over choreography for the troupes, the four successful Holt sisters, the formidable Jessie Wharton, Head Girl of the first Palace Girls and later inseparable companion to Mrs Tiller, and the most important dancer of all to John, Mary Read.

Just as Jennie had been on the sidelines while his first wife was alive, Mary became his mistress almost immediately he went through his second marriage ceremony. When he produced a new brochure he proudly placed portraits of his wife and himself side by side with his dancing sylphs. On another page he included a picture of Mary that can only be described as erotic. She was exceedingly beautiful in a childlike way. With her sensuous smile and her bare shoulders, she could be likened to a contented cat who knows she has found a good home. She came from Chorlton-on-Medlock and he created the *Sunshine* troupe around her. His wife definitely was aware of the relationship and never had a good word to say about Mary. He wisely kept the two women apart as much as possible. The *Sunshine Girls* were the only troupe to travel as far as St Petersburg and Budapest but it was noticeable that they rarely worked at the Winter Gardens which was Jennie's stronghold. In fact it was at this time just as the United States was beginning to take up his Girls that he set up a school there. He put Mary in control of the palatial establishment in New York.

Within eight years he had fully repaid his creditors and accumulated a greater fortune than ever before. He had overcome the rivalry of his son and felt that he fully deserved the expensive lifestyle he enjoyed with Mary.

Mary Read, John's mistress

Life for his Girls was less easy. Very few dancers could carry on physically beyond the age of thirty. Even had they wanted to, the producers would not have accepted them. Some never thought of planning their lives and went on dancing until no more work was offered. Going into another troupe after being a Tiller would have been too much of a comedown. The only other alternative was to start an original act but after years of 'dancing as one,' most Girls could rarely think as individuals. So at the end of their dancing career many tried desperately to hang on to the fringes of the theatre world as did matron Daisy Woodworth. Anne Liddy, the clog dancer, only worked for John for a couple of seasons, so she had not been Tillerized. She went in and out of the entertainment business all her life, one week being a top mount in an acrobatic act, and the next week working in a chocolate factory.

Many left to marry and raise families. John was always displeased when a Girl became engaged. He saw them in terms of the hours of training he had given them and regarded their departure as something to be listed in the debit columns. It was of course pure selfishness, as having persuaded the Girls to take up a short-lived career which he dominated in a exceedingly paternalistic manner, he did not remain a father figure when

54

that career was about to finish. Apart from offering a few Head Girls work as non-dancing supervisors in difficult situations abroad, there never was any long-term guidance. They were all expected to send money home to their mothers but were not taught the value of saving for their own futures. Because there was no advice whatsoever, very few saved and only later realized how foolish and extravagant they had been:

> I used to shop in Shaftesbury Avenue and buy two or three nightdresses at a time. They were so transparent and thin, you could put them through a wedding ring. I bought such beautiful, expensive clothes. I was a fool but nobody impressed on me the need to save.

As far as John was concerned the Girls did not exist once they gave up dancing. It was as if they should simply fade away when they got old like the soldiers they represented on stage. Jennie on the other hand was thrilled when the Girls announced wedding plans and there was always a warm welcome from her when they dropped in to show off a baby.

While Jane the orphan was resting she started courting a Manchester boy. She began to consider the fact that she was over twenty-one and felt anxious that she would never get a home of her own. She was torn between her love for dancing and her dreams of family life. Quite quickly she decided to marry her suitor. He became a good husband, quiet and kind, but his family were strong Methodists and were shocked that she smoked and had such a joy of life. Her outlook had been considerably broadened by her theatrical experiences. Her husband was not jealous of her dancing career but her in-laws were. When he went off to the war in 1914 she took a job as an usherette in an effort to get as near as possible to the warmth of the theatre and away from the coldness of his family. She had a tin of photographs which she would browse through, reminding herself that life had not always been so humdrum. 'Burn those,' said her sister-in-law. 'You've got to settle down; if you don't burn them, I will.' So she did as she was told. She hankered after her dancing days till she died at the age of ninety. She loved her family but having tasted a more exciting life, could not forget it.

Some Girls accepted marriage offers simply because they saw no other alternative. This became the saddest decision of all. It was the laughter and companionship that they missed more than anything when they retired. They had been geared up to use so much physical energy that even when they were very old they had a dymanic force within their bodies for which they had no outlet.

At least six lived on well into their nineties, every one of them sharing an absolute hatred of old age. All had the habit of changing the dates on the backs of their photographs to make it appear they were ten years younger than their true age. When interviewed by the author at the age of ninety-six, Edith Whalley said, 'Don't tell them how old my sister and I are, luv. After all we're Pros and Pros never tell their age.'

4

'A Pound For Me Mum . . .'

IN THE 1920s when John was regularly crossing the world to finalize his deals, he always arranged that every trip ended in New York so that he might be with his darling Mary Read. He closed his Manchester school and knowing that his wife rarely deviated from being either in Blackpool or London, he could safely assume there was little chance of a confrontation. At last he was content with his relationship with one woman; there seemed to be no others that he chose to flirt with. Because the Girls in Britain and on the Continent hardly saw him, it was a case of absence making the heart beat faster. They became terrified of him knowing that when he did appear, his object was to select one or two of the best dancers to complete troupes in America. He would not allow newcomers to be shipped abroad at random. Only the experienced with a long Tiller record were considered.

He certainly spoke his mind: 'Among you Girls, one is a star but from the dancing I've seen, the rest of you had better get back to your washtubs.'

The famous Plaza Girls. As usual, Mabel and Ethel Helliwell are the bookends

At one point Mary returned to put some of them through their paces. Having heard of her relationship with John, the Girls looked at her in fascination, and could only talk about the wonderful clothes this woman wore. She never seemed to wear the same fur coat twice.

Jennie certainly knew about the gossip and would make the odd crack. After opening nights at Blackpool, she would snub John; when he waited for her at the front entrance with their car and chauffeur she would deliberately slip out of the Stage Door and go home by tram. It must have been humiliating for her to accept that after helping him to create an empire within show business, he should choose to spend his time with a younger woman.

Despite his great wealth, John didn't miss a trick when it came to cutting the cost of exporting costumes from England. When new ones were completed, the seamstress was told to take out all used dress shields from the old costumes and stitch them into those due to be taken abroad. This saved duty.

In order to cope with the enormous workload while he was away, extra staff were taken on into the Firm as the newcomers christened it.

Although appointed as secretary, Doris Alloway became more like a daughter to Mrs Tiller. Both Jennie and John had immense compassion to the point of obsession for anyone suffering from TB. If it was known that a Girl simply had a relation with the disease, she would find herself singled out for extra help to the point of favouritism. Doris was not only the niece of a past secretary who had contracted TB, but so had both her parents.

Without exception the Girls adored Miss Doris, as she was known. Heavily built with a full round face that was always smiling, she greeted them with such warmth that even timid newcomers relaxed. She mothered all of them in a way that Jennie could not now she was becoming more erratic. She worked a sixteen-hour day, returning to the flat where she often stayed with Jennie and Jessie. For some unknown reason, the blinds were always drawn, giving it a depressing atmosphere. Many found it oppressive. Dispensing love and friendship to everyone she met, she was almost too good to be true. Faced with the need to chastise a dancer, she never gave way to anger nor showed her annoyance but her eyes would fill with tears and she would say, 'I never thought a Tiller would let us down like this.' Everyone appreciated her saintlike qualities and loved her.

Although the accounts were handled by a well-known firm, there were in addition a mountain of wage packets and simple book-keeping to be handled. At last John's son Robert was given a chance; he was allowed to take over this clerical work, and was methodical enough to cope with it. He certainly needed a helping hand. He had been badly injured in the war, staying in hospital for four years and undergoing twenty-eight operations. Despite his heavy family commitments, he was instantly dismissed by his father when it was discovered that he had entertained a nurse in the company flat.

Robert Smith was a relative of John's first wife and found himself summoned by the great man to take over the accounts. 'Mr Smith', as he was always formally addressed, was under the impression he was just temporary holiday relief. On hearing that the job was to be permanent he was gallant enough to ask Robert's sanction before accepting. On learning the reason for his predecessor's dismissal he decided never to put his livelihood at risk by getting friendly with any of the Girls. He vowed that no hint of scandal would ever be attached to him. In a business that was headed by someone virtually at war with his entire family over their moral misdemeanours, this was a wise decision and brought Mr Smith fifty years' work.

Gently but firmly he asserted himself in the organization. When requested to do his work in the company flat, and remembering the funereal atmosphere of the place, he refused. He realized that accepting it as an office would have meant being pressed into staying late at night talking shop. He demanded and got a proper office. At first it seemed impossible to cope with two employers with their contrasting attitudes towards money. John was prudent; his wife reckless. As they were rarely in the office together, he found his orders constantly changing. Eventually he told them he could not serve two masters and as he had, by then, proved himself to Tiller, he was given complete financial control.

The Carlton Girls, one of the many Tiller troupes who worked on the exhausting ciné-variety circuits

The Carlton Tiller Girls

One of Mr Smith's regular jobs was to send an agreed proportion of the Girls' wages to their mothers. 'A pound for me Mum, a pound for me digs and a pound for me.' He would smile to himself every time he heard this as they came to sign their contracts. Mr Smith understood there was a need to send money home to most mothers but reasoned if the Girls were capable of earning above average wages, they should be treated like adults and make their own decisions about their finances. So from then on they learnt the discipline of budgeting and faithfully sent home the pound themselves.

The office was more like an army headquarters than a theatrical business as every day Girls would be transported somewhere at home or abroad. There were no worries when entire troupes toured as their Captains were always experienced travellers but often one or two replacements were needed and they had to travel in couples or even alone. The paternalistic Tillers knew they would be at risk so William was taken on to carry out these arrangements.

No one ever seemed to know William's surname and he had a bizarre appearance at a time when smartness was highly valued. Most people thought he looked like a tramp with his habit of tying his trousers up with string, but the first thing that all the dancers noticed was that he had big, flat feet. Very tall, usually wearing a cap and carrying a basket on each arm, he was a real trouper to all of them. He not only met them off trains, got taxis, and frequently turned up at theatres to see how they were getting on, but would also dip into one of his baskets and present each Girl with a bar of chocolate. If Jennie ordered baths to be taken it was William who escorted them, gave them soap and a towel and waited for them to come out. The fact that he seemed a little simple did not escape their notice but they felt such affection for him that no one ever teased him. The other members of staff knew that his apparent simpleness was due to a sad childhood; he had been brutally beaten by his father and this had resulted in his withdrawing into himself. He had a great love of music and when the rehearsal rooms were rented out would join the musicians. He was jointly responsible for writing at least one tune which became a hit and made a name for the other writer. Typically he was never given acknowledgement for his part in its creation.

The Theatre Royal, Leeds, 1923: Doris Carter (top row, second left) appeared in the same line as her aunt, Gertie Whalley (front row, left). Nellie of the Knobbles is in the top row (third left)

As well as rehearsing the Girls Jessie Wharton now became companion to Mrs Tiller. After her spell in the Palace Girls she had graduated to playing small parts in the Blackpool shows. Now that she was too old to dance regularly she would understudy the Girls and they all recognized her as a marvellous dancer:

I'll say I remember Jessie Wharton, she was a real trouper. She used to wear a spotless white blouse with an enormous black bow on her chest and always wore her rehearsal pants very long. If you ever put on long knickers, the others used to call them your 'Jessie Wharton's'.

Another ex-Head Girl who now taught was Nellie Nixon, commonly called Nellie of the Knobbles because she was so thin that her muscles stood out.

Lily O'Grady hated the squalor and untidiness of the dressing-rooms

At about this time tights were no longer worn on stage: 'wet white' was used for the Girls' legs. This was made up by the Head Girl mixing together oxide of zinc, glycerine, rosewater, a touch of yellow ochre and methylated spirits, the latter helping to dry it on the legs. Naturally it had to be washed off after the show before outdoor clothes were put on. There would be a frantic dive for the wash-basins as soon as the show finished, as most theatres still only had one basin in dressing-rooms that held well over a dozen Girls. The wash down would be done with one leg up at a time and an impatient queue waiting behind.

All the difficulties with 'wet white' were eliminated in Birmingham where there was an obscure ruling that bare legs were banned (this remained in force as late as the 1950s), so when playing there they were given cotton tights but had to put a penny at the side, wrap a piece of string round it and the tights in order to hold them up. Being so unused to all this, most preferred to literally stick with the 'wet white'.

Greasepaint was now used for the face. Gone was the flattened-out effect; a more contoured look was possible with these sticks that could be bought from chemists all over the country. The numerous shades were indicated by numbers. The Girls used a combination of numbers five and nine; a few streaks painted on the cheeks, chin, nose and forehead were blended with the fingertips. Eyes were accentuated with blue shadow for the lids and a red blob in the corner. A special carmine stick replaced rouge on the cheeks followed by a dusting of face powder. Their eyelashes were still built up with hot black, mouth open to concentrate. The whole ritual took most of them half an hour though there were always a few that gossiped so much they had to be nagged by their Head Girl. Because their new make-up was so much thicker, a strong removal cream was needed to take it off. Boiled lard in a pan of water, cooled, strained and mixed with oil of lavender was used. This gooey mess was wiped off with towels at the end of the evening.

In England at that time shop girls would have a weekly wage of about twenty-five shillings so John Tiller was giving dancers an excellent deal by paying them fifty shillings a week when on tour, matinées providing an extra ten shillings. They would only spend ten shillings towards their rooms, which they shared. Another ten shillings was put aside for food; they rarely learnt to cook as landladies preferred to prepare the food the Girls had bought.

Touring was tough. Each weekend would see them on their way. One Girl said:

Your life seemed to be spent sitting on skips at Crewe. When you got to the station you'd see groups of theatricals. You'd know the pros, they'd have their round hat boxes, their big fur collars, the chorus would all be together, they always wore those high heeled shoes with bows at the front. It was such a laugh, so many theatricals all diving into the buffet.

As each train arrived you would see the reservation stickers on the coaches. *Desert Song, More Splashes Revue*. Yes that was more like it, you had a friend in that so you ran along the train trying to find her. All around you, others would be shrieking 'darling', kissing each other on the cheek. Always so many darlings, and you knew they hated each other.

The daft thing was they were probably going back to where we'd been working. Seemed pointless all this travelling.

Another was more practical:

> The main thing you wanted to do on the train was pull the blinds down, wash your stockings and put your hair in curlers.

The Girls were lucky if they had booked digs, otherwise a visit to the stage door-keeper was made and he would probably have the list. Failing that they had to trudge down the nearest side streets with their suitcases, knock on doors at random asking whether they took theatricals. By the twenties, lace curtains and an aspidistra in the window were bad omens. The owner would inevitably be old-fashioned, strict about everything, and there would be no chance of a front door key each.

The Carlton Tiller Girls.

The Carlton Girls in another routine

Peggy Price hoots with laughter at the sort of women who put on airs in front of her lodgers:

> They used to try to be so posh. I used to play up to that, pretend to be the lady. One of them asked if I would like some beetroot. I said that I didn't care for it. 'Oh, my son loves beetroot butties,' she replied.

Another time my friend and I were in bed, I heard the woman shout, 'Are the two ladies in bed yet?' 'Yes, Ma,' was the reply. 'Well, let our Jimmy down to pee in the sink then.'

Once we were sitting round the table and the landlady's son said, 'Give me the butter.' She pulled herself upright very grandly. 'If what?' she asked, waiting for him to say please. 'If you're not too bloody busy to get it,' was his answer.

Digs were notoriously bad in London and in desperation the mother of the actress Fay Compton founded a hostel called The Theatre Girls' Home in Greek Street, Soho. It was an admirable venture and most of the Girls found it an exciting place to stay. All theatre and film calls were thoughtfully put on the noticeboard. The management often let their regulars stay on credit, within reason. It was very strict, which pleased parents and the Tiller office. Certainly no boyfriends were permitted to call on the boarders. Not that the Girls wanted them to as during rehearsals they were utterly exhausted. Said Mary Fox:

I found muscles I never knew existed. I couldn't even walk up the stairs. I used to have to go up on my bottom. Not only were boyfriends forbidden but even fathers were not allowed to cross the threshold to carry their daughter's suitcases in.

The Girls slept in cubicles with others, which seemed strange at first but the fun they generated helped to overcome any homesickness. After about nine months' stay they could graduate to a single room but by then many preferred to be in with their friends. The charge was incredibly low, only a pound a week and all food provided except butter. In those early days they were expected to go to chapel every morning; bells seemed to announce every change in the timetable. There was a big rehearsal room for those capable of working in the evening and a nice sitting-room for those who could not. While at the hostel they could get a free pass to visit any cinema or theatre so a decent life was possible on the half pay rehearsal salary.

Mrs Tiller took a lease on a flat in the Bloomsbury area. She had the walls repapered, new carpets and furniture bought for every room and then sub-let it to her favourite Girls. As the Helliwell sisters always had the pick of the best jobs, they of course lived there while working in London. There were four of them so there was as much chance of the average Girl staying at the Tiller flat as of getting into Buckingham Palace.

The war had been over a long time. Titles for productions now mirrored the jazz era: *Sparks of Wit and Flashes of Humour, Tit Bits from Tip Top, Life and Laughter.* The flappers had reached Blackpool. Tiller writing the storyline still whisked his audience round the world but the comedy element was more dominant. A working motor car was featured on stage in one scene. The songs too had jokier titles: *Down Where the Cross-Eyed Claras Grow, I'm the Good Man that Was so Hard to Find.*

John was rarely seen in Blackpool; after he had written the outline for the summer show he put assistant directors in charge of rehearsals. When he did appear, just before opening night he looked an impressive figure in his expensive clothes. He became quite frightening when he got in a rage trying to explain his last minute ideas:

> We went on for what seemed like hours and still none of us understood. Eventually he bent over and told the Head Girl to kick him; she was amazed but she did so — just stepped forward and kicked him and that was exactly the step he wanted. They call it the strut now.
> Another time he got us to lie on the floor with our legs in the air. We wondered what on earth was happening. With his hands he showed us where he wanted the legs to go. It was simple but effective. We stayed on the floor throughout the routine with our legs up — didn't half hurt.

Looking more like rugger forwards, the local Girls line up for 'On the Road' at the Winter Gardens, Blackpool, 1924

Up to this point, variety had been the main source of income for the Firm. Now the public were beginning to prefer the new ciné-variety as a

form of entertainment because it was such good value. For the bargain price of one shilling and sixpence the audience could watch alternating film and stage shows. There would be three to five showings a day depending on the degree of popularity. Very often a second film and newsreel would be interspersed with more acts and an organist.

American companies decided to build new cinemas in Britain and as the reputation of the Girls had already been made in the States, they were eager to book Tiller troupes. The various lines of dancers took the prefix of the cinema building they were appearing in. As a result the *Paramount Tillers* rehearsed in their red and white check rompers, the *Carltons* in brown and white, the *Plazas* in blue and white and the *Astorias* in yellow and white. The whole country seemed to be full of Tiller Girls kicking in their little check outfits. There were even handkerchiefs in various colour schemes and embroidered with the troupe's name.

Meanwhile the Palace Girls c.1923 now contained some of John's favourite and prettiest Girls

Previous theatre work had been tiring but now ciné-variety was exhausting. A successful film usually ran for six weeks and there were three to five separate performances, six days a week to get through. A newcomer could be excused for not realizing in what show she was performing. The day began at 10 am for rehearsals for the next production but if this proved unsuccessful, it was taken off and the new production rushed on. As ciné-variety rapidly increased in popularity, smaller cinemas presented similar shows and the Tiller office was inundated with bookings for their troupes. Instead of resting in dressing-rooms between shows, the Girls were burnt out coping with double and tripling. Coaches would transport them from place to place, their costumes hanging above their heads. Often they would change on the move.

John provided the Plaza management with two different lines of Girls with no particular style, then he hit upon the idea of creating a line of tall Girls with long legs. The *Plazas* immediately took the public's imagination. Suddenly everyone wanted tall dancers. It was the beginning of the end for many short Tillers who had started work as juveniles, reaping the reward of looking much younger than their years.

Francis Mangon, an inventive lighting designer, had been brought over from America to be in charge of productions for the Plaza company. Most of the visual ideas were imported but he found Ethel Helliwell brilliant at organizing the execution of them. So began a relationship on and off stage that gave the audiences some of the finest Tiller work.

The driving force behind the Plazas was undoubtedly Ethel; to some extent she relished knowing that the Girls called her the slave driver behind her back:

One mistake and we were in next day for two hours. I suppose it was good for us, but we didn't think so at the time.

For her part she was under extreme pressure, still only in her twenties and supervising up to 160 Girls at any one point. Deeply in love with Francis Mangon, she was anxious to impress him professionally. He reciprocated by flaunting his other affairs in her face.

The Plaza Girls, a troupe of tall dancers that were an instant hit with the public. Ethel Helliwell is appropriately stationed at the top

One routine that all troupes performed was the Pony Trot. Created by John way back in 1910, it began with the Girls grouped in sets of four dressed as ponies and imitating the animals' movements. Before they became accustomed to the heavy weight of the head-dresses, they felt as though their heads would drop off. They would curse their lack of height as they pranced round because the tallest Girls were always chosen as 'drivers' and simply trotted behind. Each set of four had their reins held by a 'driver', so once on stage there was no way that a message could be passed to a colleague should anything go amiss. This problem was to make it the most accident-prone routine in Tiller history. They were literally held together in sickness and health. One Head Girl found her team circling round the stage once as rehearsed but then galloping straight off stage to the lavatories; apparently one of the Girls had realized that she had a sudden attack of diarrhoea and had acted with unheard-of initiative.

In the 1950s Bert Hardy brilliantly captured the essence of the Pony Trot for *Picture Post* but the re-creation of the routine shown on television at that time seemed a pale version of the original to the women of the twenties; they recall the music being so much more inventive with a man simulating the horses' hooves with coconut shells, hunting horns and whiplashes all adding to the atmosphere.

When film companies wanted troupes, the office gave the work to those already appearing in the London theatres — the lucky ones in *Raise the Roof, A Little Bit of Fluff, Charley's Aunt* and *Life and Laughter* with Tom Walls, Ralph Lynn and Syd Chaplin. They found their combined film and theatre schedule as exhausting as ciné-variety. They were up at 5 am to travel by train to Elstree to get there by 7 am. They would then find that they were hanging around for hours and the crafty ones would try to find a prop bed to catch up on some sleep. As soon as they finished around 5 pm, they would travel back to London and snatch a meal of the inevitable egg and chips. After that it was on to the theatre for the evening show, then back to the Theatre Girls' Club for, if they are to be believed, another meal of egg and chips. The extra pound a day for their film work did little to compensate for their tiredness which surely must have been as much due to under-nourishment as overwork.

The Plaza troupe were delighted with themselves. A critic had coined a phrase for them and it was taken up as a catch phrase — 'They dance as one woman and what a woman.' Whilst they were appearing in *Up With the Lark* at the Adelphi Theatre, they coped admirably with their filming schedule but were furious when Sickert produced a picture of them called *High Steppers*. He had the habit of hoarding newspaper cuttings that interested him and occasionally created a picture from one. The Girls regarded this one with loathing as it shows them with heads and legs all at different angles.

One of the Plaza Girls bore the surname of Tiller. In fact her audition must have created deep turmoil in John. She was the daughter of John's estranged cousin, Samuel and his wife Marie Millward, one of his favourite principals. When Sam died in 1923 aged only fifty-four, Marjorie felt free to try to do what she had always wanted, and auditioned for the Tillers:

My father died when I was fifteen. The following year, in May, I sneaked off to audition for Tiller without my mother's knowledge. I had to wait two hours before seeing him as he was in conference with a producer. Funnily enough Doris Alloway didn't ask for my name. Finally he took me in to his office and said he was looking for Girls to work at the Winter Gardens, Blackpool. I auditioned and he hired me. I thanked him and was about to leave when he realized he didn't know my name. I wouldn't tell him until he assured me three times that I had the job.

He got the shock of his life when he found out who I was and asked if my mother knew I was there. When I said she didn't, he rang for his chauffeur and told me he was going to see her and asked if I wanted to go with him.

I thought I was in enough trouble so I refused. Off he went; he must have persuaded my mother because when I eventually did get home, she didn't put up any resistance. I don't think they had contracts in those days; I certainly was never given one to sign.

Marjorie never felt that there was any favouritism shown to her. In fact she felt that Jennie positively disliked her, particularly when none of the shoes in stock fitted her and Jennie refused to buy her a new pair. Dancing night after night in a pair of shoes a size too small regularly reminded her of Jennie's animosity. In truth through the years Tiller Girls danced in ill-fitting shoes and had bunions to prove it for the rest of their lives.

After a few weeks in Blackpool, Marjorie was overjoyed when sent to America to join the *Lollipop Troupe* for a year. She returned to another season at the Winter Gardens in 1925. John as usual attended the opening night. Afterwards he met Marjorie at the stage door and said, 'I want you to know I'm well pleased with your work. I have great things in store for you which I will tell you about when I come back from America.'

She was never to learn of his plans as he sailed for New York the next day and never returned. He died on 21st October, 1925, of angina pectoris in Lennox Hill Hospital, New York.

In his obituary in *The Stage,* the writer pertinently remarked that 'People die not so much on account of their age or that they are worn out, but because of the loss of their lifelong associates.' It was a strange coincidence that he made his final sailing to America on the day that his closest friend, Mr Huddlestone, was buried.

The obituaries published in Britain, on the Continent and in America all acknowledged him as the originator of military precision dancing and reported how he had dominated a whole era of show business. They also stated that his kind regard for his employees was unique in the entertainment world.

John seemed to sense death approaching. He had made a will only one month before and when Mr Smith reminded him that the lease of the office premises was due for renewal, he remarked that he wouldn't be needing them. The previous year he had disposed of all his costumes, props and scenery. It certainly seemed as though he was tying up all the loose ends of his life.

His body was brought over from New York by Mary Read and fifty

Girls representing troupes all over the country met at Westminster Bridge Road and had the strange experience of travelling in the Necropolis Funeral train to Brookwood Cemetery. Despite the sadness of the occasion, many gave way to hysterical giggling as they gradually realized that every compartment contained mourners or corpses. They sobered up at the graveside in anticipation of the encounter of Jennie and Mary but it was not as hostile as they expected. Later as a memorial to their husbands, Mrs Huddlestone and Jennie presented a stained glass window at the church at St Stephens-on-the-Cliff at Blackpool.

When his will was published, the popular press were delighted to highlight the acrimony that John expressed in it. 'Father Rebukes Sons' ran the headlines. The bewildered children of his son Robert learnt for the first time how their apparently benevolent grandfather really viewed their father. 'I have made no provision for my son Robert other than the bequest of £100 because he has been the recipient of my bounty during my lifetime and has nevertheless caused me sorrow and trouble on numerous occasions.'

Speculation about the relationship between Lawrence and John was also at an end. Kind souls, such as Mr Smith, who had reckoned that Tiller

Just before he died, John persuaded Jennie to go on holiday. For once she is not dressed all in black

69

John never forgave Lawrence for breaking away and going into competition with him. Lawrence copied his father and started with groups of juveniles such as these *Merritots*

had encouraged his son to set up on his own, were proved wrong. John wrote emphatically: 'I have made no provision for my son Lawrence other than the bequest of £100 because he had his own business in opposition to mine; I was willing to work with him and help him but he would not and preferred competition.'

Jennie was heard to remark that the will was a cruel one; by this she meant that not only were family recriminations made public but that when outlining a request for a company to be formed, her husband certainly showed his doubts about her competence. He suggested that the directors be restricted to Mr Smith, Mary Read and Doris Alloway. Even more humiliating was his belief that Mary, not Jennie, should be made president and managing director. There was at least a proviso that she should be asked for her written consent before the company was set up but otherwise she was not mentioned in his plans for the future of the schools.

He named just six of his favourite Head Girls and awarded them shares, which must have surprised others who thought they were special in his affections. Mary of course was to get the largest amount — twenty. Rene Todd, the second in command in New York got ten, as did Doris Birch, the top Girl in Paris and also Nellie of the Knobbles fame. The redoubtable Ethel must have been shocked when it was made clear she was down-graded to five, the same as Gracie Holt. Kind, gentle William received acknowledgement for his loyalty and he too was awarded five.

The fact that John had handed over the reins of power to Miss Doris and Mr Smith seemed a great honour but his stipulation that they should keep and maintain the name and reputation of the business so long as it was possible to do so proved a massive task for them in later years.

Despite John's wishes, when the company was finally registered only Jennie and Doris Alloway were listed as directors with Mr Smith as secretary. Mary had been totally excluded. Jennie had won. The completion had taken two weary years. As Mr Smith admitted: 'It was anything for a quiet life,' and Jennie had her way.

The Tiller reputation kept the business alive; despite the fact that Jennie did not have her husband's inspiration to create new routines, she certainly had the character to head the organization. After John died, when the Girls were asked to appear at the Royal Command Performance, she saw no reason why this show should be any different from the others and stood in her usual place at the side of the stage, hissing corrections at the Girls.

5

'Paris, of Course'

WE started to rehearse our routine for the show. Mrs Tiller suddenly pulled me out and made me stand at the side. She said nothing to me and after rehearsals I was still standing there; I'd done nothing all morning, and she called me into the office. I was scared to death, really I thought I'd got the push.

'Well,' she said, 'do you want to go?'

'Where, Mrs Tiller?'

'Paris, of course.'

Well, that was it and I was in a daze. I had to get my passport done, my parents' written permission because I was only seventeen and I found myself in Paris two days later.

This was typical of the casual way in which Jennie selected Girls to go abroad. It became a pattern to work in Paris after a season or two in England but if a replacement was urgently needed, any dancer who caught her attention was likely to be shipped abroad. To this day Girls who worked in the 1920s would not consider others to be proper Tillers unless they had done the inevitable Paris stint.

For Jennie, it was just another date to be filled. Elyse Burton said:

I remember crying my eyes out. I was only sixteen; they wouldn't let me go on a world tour. I went into her office crying.

'Look, love,' she said, 'how would you like to go to Paris? Would you be happy if you went there? Would you stop crying?' I did and I went.

Jennie recognized that the world could be at any of her Girls' feet but she also understood that sometimes the youngsters were too scared to travel abroad. They had no idea what was in store for them; their education was basic and there was no television to enlarge their horizons. The cinema shed a little light on the way of life in America but to them the continent was an unknown place with unintelligible languages.

I thought I was going into a different world when I entered Germany. 'Oh look, there's an English cow,' I said. I really thought it would look different.

Tiller had no sympathy; he would actively show his dislike for anyone who rejected foreign contracts. He now regarded the British work simply as training for the more lucrative engagements abroad.

I had rehearsed all the routine for the South America job, then I just got a bit panicky; the captain tried to talk me back into it. Tiller was mad; he never forgave me but Jennie just said, 'Perhaps Bella doesn't want to go so far away.' She understood.

All Girls under twenty-one had to get written permission from their parents and although fathers still tended to be against the idea, no one appeared to have committed forgery. Many a family row lasted for days until the dancer got her way. To add to the stigma of the wicked stage, the men also feared that their daughters would end up on the streets of Paris. As usual the mothers were all for the idea of travel:

The aptly named *Extraordinary Dancers* who were booked to appear in the highly sophisticated Folies-Bergère and then went on to tour the world

73

My mother thought we could see the world which she never would do, that it would be an education in itself. She was far-sighted in that way.

The troupe called the *Eight Extraordinary Dancers* travelled together in an outdoor uniform that had been supplied: heavy capes, white socks, boots, and, as a symbol of their destination — a beret. It was an exceptionally youthful group, five of them were only fourteen, and the fact that they were booked for, of all places, the highly sophisticated Folies-Bergère made the 'extraordinary' very apt. Because of their age, they were cosseted more than usual and Mr Smith escorted them to the boat and bought them dinner.

If they travelled alone or in couples, it was of course dear William who met them, carried their luggage, bought their tickets, but once at the docks, they would have to do the rest of the trip alone. The only advice from Miss Doris was to follow the crowd. Despite the risks involved no one was lost or waylaid. Doris Lupton remembers her first trip vividly:

My friend and I bought new coats before we went. Black lisle stockings and flat-heeled shoes. We must have looked so gormless; we certainly looked it in our passport photos. We went in to see Jennie before we left.

'Oh look, Jessie,' she said. 'They've even got their gloves on. You know, Girls, all ladies wear gloves!' And to this day I can't go shopping without my gloves on.

The sophisticated appearance of the other Girls was miraculously achieved on a salary of around £4 a week. They longed for the hats and shoes they saw in the Galeries Lafayette. As they could not afford *haute couture* they went to a little shop opposite their theatre which was called Mama's and the owner allowed them to put money aside weekly to buy the dresses they wanted.

A tallyman or woman visited their dressing-rooms with exquisitely embroidered lingerie which they found impossible to resist. They were a captive audience for the beautiful satin and silk and a few weeks later their mothers would be complaining to Mr Smith that their weekly pound had not been received.

It was usual for the Girls to stay at the English Girls' Club when they first arrived. Learning to pronounce the address 'Quatorze rue du Perre, Place Pigalle' to a taxi driver was the first hurdle they had to overcome:

I had a terrible job. I'd say it over and over again in my schoolgirl French. He'd just give me a look, the way the French do and eventually when I was thoroughly humiliated, he would repeat it properly.

The Club was run by an Englishman, the Rev F.A. Cardew, on the same lines as its twin establishment in Soho. Here there were dormitories for four or six and just as in hospital wards of the time, the walls were painted a sombre grey. Each inmate had her own locker and a screen for privacy. When the Prince of Wales was in Paris, they heard that he would be visiting the Club. 'I don't know what the Prince will think of these bare walls', Ann East said to her room-mates. She persuaded them to invest in ten rolls of wallpaper bought from a corner shop that sold everything from paraffin to knickers. Unfortunately despite the wide range, the stock did not include paste so they were up until the early hours, matching and fastening the wallpaper on with drawing pins.

Inside and outside the English Girls' Club in Paris. Here the John and Lawrence Tiller Girls met but kept their distance

The *Eight Extraordinary Dancers* lived there up to the ears as usual with their own brand of juvenile mischief, watching the matron getting undressed by looking over her partition or stitching up her nightdress. At one point they were thought to look peaky so each was given a bottle of Guinness and some oysters and they sat on their little iron beds scoffing them. A vision of the Infant Phenomenon multiplied by eight.

After they had proved their trustworthiness, permission would be given for them to live in couples in a *pension*. This decison divided the independent types from the gregarious; some thoroughly enjoyed staying at the hostel for years:

I loved the Club and all the Girls. It was my cup of tea. I loved fooling around. I hated the idea of being on my own.

Being so conditioned to being together at all times, even after some Girls moved out they returned every day to play cards.

The Englishness of the place suited most Tillers; terrified of unknowingly swallowing horsemeat in restaurants, many preferred to suffer cold rice pudding at the Club. They were also put off the idea of French food by smelling garlic on the stagehands' breath. The combined smell of garlic and eau de cologne was terrible.

Also staying at the Club were the Lawrence Tiller Girls. The family tension between father and son was passed down to the dancers. There was no ruling that they should not talk to each other but that is what they believed. To this day many are convinced they were kept in separate dining rooms.

Four of the *Eight Extraordinary Dancers* performing the 'Pony Trot'

John was paid an annual fee by the Folies-Bergère management for the exclusive use of his Girls in Paris. Forty-eight were used in one production and of these the *Eight Extraordinary Dancers* did their own specialities which were naturally very juvenile: the *Pony Trot,* the *Bells* and the *Xylophone.* The remaining taller dancers, called *Les John Tiller Folies Stars*, not only appeared in the production numbers with the rest of the cast but also had their own numbers. Working on the stage of the Folies was fraught with difficulty — there were so many trap doors for the various effects: fountains, moving staircases, foam cascading down the side, even mimosa perfume sprayed from the flies in one number. They

Ah! Les jambes de la femme!

77

wondered why they were asked if they could stand heights and naturally no one admitted to such a weakness so seven volunteers were picked to appear in *Les Jambes de la Femme*. They had to take their places on a enormous swing; once seated it was lowered from the flies until the audience could only see their legs as they went through their act.

There was an effective underwater scene which entailed the Girls walking in fours into a lake and appearing to drown. In fact once submerged they had to find a red rod and drag themselves along it to the other side of the stage; more than one mother screamed in fear when she saw the show. Considerably less risky but with definite romantic potential was the *Kisses Over the Garden Wall* number, the entire line being dressed as either girls or boys. At the end, the 'boys' clambered onto the wall, sat with legs crossed and threw themselves backwards over the wall one by one into the arms of a stagehand. Not one Girl was dropped and due to the anti-social breath of the stagehands, not one romance developed.

The star of the Folies in 1926/7 was the irrepressible Josephine Baker. She was friendly, which was unusual for stars of the day. She could not believe her eyes when she saw the Tillers being marched off in the crocodile line to the English Girls' Club after rehearsals. They were equally amazed at her. It was unbelievable that she was only the same age as many of them. They had heard about her erotic exploits but their jaws dropped during the dress rehearsal of one of her entrances. Half nude, she held onto a big, round glass ball which was slowly lowered from the flies and poised above the stalls. They were even more agog during the much publicized *Banana Dance* when she danced with only a curtain of bananas round her waist. Another time she seemed to have nothing on under a grass skirt as she danced on a mirrored floor.

They were filled with admiration for her highly individual personality; they had been trained to sink their personalities into the line and were happy to do so. Although they were in the same show and of the same age, they were a world apart as women and performers. She gave them an understanding of the qualities needed to become a star.

As far as nudity was concerned they quickly accepted it in Josephine's act as it seemed such a natural part of her but their attitudes were quite prudish when confronted with the nudes backstage. There seemed to be a surfeit at the Folies. While waiting to go on, they would see the women rub lipstick onto their fingers from their lips and transfer it onto their navels and nipples. Working alongside such eroticism made them feel awkward. They were proud to be in the show but terrified that their parents would send for them if they knew of such blatant nudity. So they spent hours painting brassières onto the nude photographs before sending the souvenir programme home. However, when Dolly Howard thought she would peep through the curtains to see how her father was reacting to the nudes she found that she was the one who was shocked. He had his binoculars on them! Among the English there were two opinions about the French girls. One group swore that they did not get any salary, but took the job to attract men for prostitution; and others went out of their way to prove their own sophistication by talking to them. All agreed they had a rough deal as their work often involved great pain. Appearing in the *Living Curtain* meant that their arms were strapped in an outstretched

DOROTHY FROSTICK.

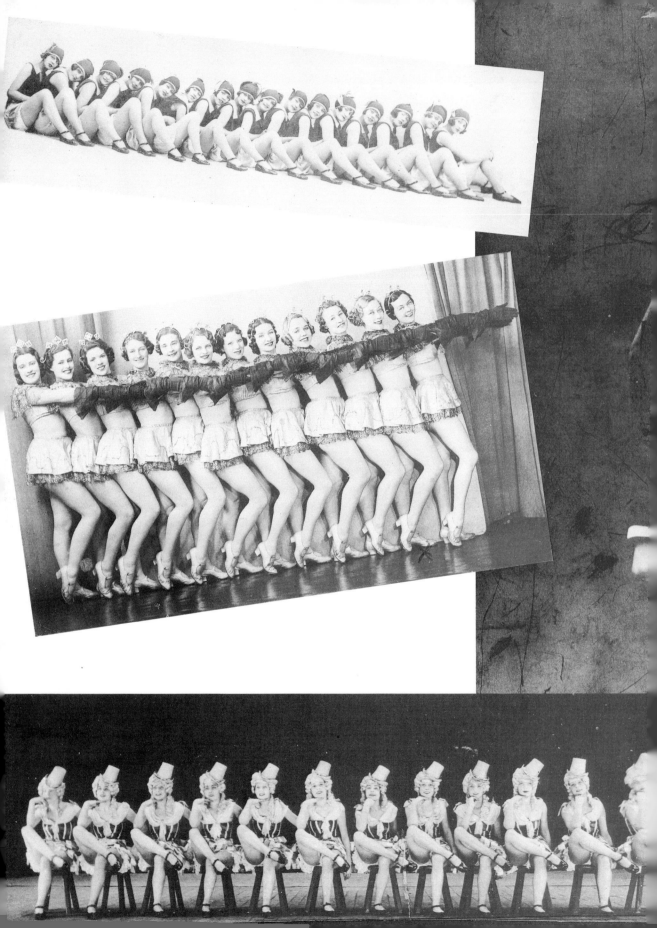

Maybe this records the Girls'
first sighting of the nudes!

position from the interval until the finale. Often one of them would faint
and be left prostrate until the end. They could be friendly:

She took a great fancy to me, used to buy me presents. I thought this
was marvellous. They weren't expensive gifts; a little posy, perfume.
Then she suggested that I go and stay with her in her flat. I thought that

was wonderful. I'd save lots of money as I wouldn't have to pay for digs. When I told the Head Girl, she explained that the French girl was a lesbian.

Well, that didn't mean a thing to me, so she took me out next day to the Champs Elysée, into a very expensive shop. There was a woman buying some lingerie for another. The Head Girl warned that the same fate would happen to me.

I was intrigued, I still couldn't see what was wrong with having your underwear bought for you. Then I heard there was a book about this lesbianism. I got it and was shocked. Even so I smuggled it home to England just because it was banned.

Also working in Paris were the Lawrence Tiller Girls

The Head Girl who was so anxious to shepherd Mary back to heterosexuality was Doris Birch. She had lived in Paris so long that she had the appearance of a true Parisienne with her neatly bobbed hair, her brogues and long cigarette holder, inhaling the smoke as though she wanted it to reach her toes. She had a highly charged emotional life, two-timing a *Paris Wire* journalist with a jockey who beat her up. This probably accounted for the fact that she was not on duty at the theatre as much as she should have been and was very moody when she was there.

Once the show was on, life was fairly easy with one show a night lasting from 8 till 11.30 pm seven days a week, and matinées on Saturdays and Sundays. During their time off, there was an exciting world to explore for the adventurous. A few developed a liking for the racecourse and as it had been drummed into them to dress correctly for every occasion, somehow they managed to provide themselves with the obligatory long trailing gowns by lending each other clothes and accessories; they appreciated the elegance of their suave escorts in tail coats and top hats.

Official invitations to all *les Girls* would be pinned up on the stage doorkeeper's noticeboard. As their popularity grew, they became quite blasé when deciding what to accept. It was the height of the nightclub era and naturally the owners were eager for the presence of the attractive dancers who had been delighting their members earlier in the evening.

One night several arrived in response to a typical invitation. They found the gentlemen in the club in white tie and tails all smoking through long cigarette holders, as was the fashion. Thankfully none of them tried the 'feely feely' business that the Girls loathed. It was true they were very quiet which the Girls thought was a combination of shyness and the language barrier. As they left they received a kiss on their hands. Next morning the stage manager took great pleasure in informing them they had been to a women-only club. Barbara Sutton was stunned:

> I still didn't really understand when he said they were lesbians. I thought it was a nationality and went round saying I'd met some strange women from Lesbia.

A couple had more facts of life shown to them by a taxidriver. Although it meant a detour he drove them through the Bois du Boulogne. He knew where the nocturnal gatherings were held:

> The first time was a bit of a shock. He went through quietly with his lights off and then suddenly switched them on. We learnt quite a bit.

Strategy was necessary to get out on a date alone. The under-sixteens would be marshalled back in crocodile fashion by an older Girl of about twenty-six. The matron of the Club was under strict orders from both the London office and the Rev F.A. Cardew to keep a rigorous check on her charges. In order to get official night leave, one successful plot was to pretend to have a brother or an uncle, depending on the prospective escort's age, who was supposedly visiting Paris. With luck the senior Girl would tell them precisely what they could or could not do, and when they had to return to the Club. The most open arrangement was to inform a rich suitor that if he wanted a date, he would have to take the whole troupe out. This was a popular move as it guaranteed no 'feely feely'. Surprisingly the men were always delighted to take up the offer.

The Girls dared each other to go out with boys of their own age: after all they had to find out what a 'French kiss' entailed. When they escaped with these younger, more eligible men, they loved to go to the bistros and discover French food. A meal would only cost five francs but they noticed how the prices went up if their escorts were American, English or Australian. Bowls of fruit, flowers, even the cruet would have to be paid for. They enjoyed the Moulin Rouge and Bal Tabarin, the club that presented a Russian act:

> We used to see them dancing. A knife here, a knife there. It would stick in between their toes, it looked so easy. In the cellars, absinthe was all the rage, one sip and you felt as though your head would come off.
>
> A few were unfortunate, they fell in love with Russians. Wasn't there something wrong with Russia at any time? Anyway, they would fall in love with these Counts who were ten a penny and even pay for their drinks. I warned them.

For every Tiller that admits to sneaking out, two will insist that they stayed indoors every night. They all say there were no passionate affairs but occasionally the tempters must have been successful. It is unlikely we shall ever know what some really got up to. The famous Tiller discretion was instilled into them at the same time as their routines and with equal thoroughness.

The Tiller organization lost the Folies booking a couple of years after John's death but other work was soon offered in Paris by the Paramount cinema group. It was on ciné-variety lines and as the producer was Francis Mangon, he naturally brought over Ethel Helliwell to choreograph for him.

Whilst they were doing five shows a day and rehearsing at the Paramount, they were told to double at the Lido. This was in the heart of the Champs Elysées and was a subterranean establishment consisting of a swimming pool, a Turkish bath and a cabaret:

> We must have been going round like zombies. It was like a nightclub at the Lido. A very handsome place, a dance floor and a wonderful swimming pool. On it were gondolas and beautiful-looking men punting the show girls.
>
> The Turkish baths were quite near our dressing-rooms and we must have been so exhausted one night that we lost our way. We suddenly found ourselves in the Turkish baths with a dozen nude men. I don't know who was the most surprised.

The Paramount/Lido schedule was one of the most exhausting a Tiller line ever had to endure. After a few months the Girls would be sent to perform in casinos, mainly dotted round the south of France and Monte Carlo. Although they still did an average of three shows a night, after their stint in Paris this was easy. It felt strange to be working so close to their audiences. The stage area at the casino in Le Touquet was almost close enough to the tables to kick the glasses off. Many of the musicians were unused to working with dancers and once when the band was out of tempo, the Girls started singing as they danced to get the music synchronized. For the second show their Captain stood by the pianist and rapped out the rhythm.

The glamour of Monte Carlo was renowned so they were overjoyed when a troupe was summoned from England to appear in a special show for Prince Rainier's father at the Opera House. Their billing announced

The strangest setting for a Tiller routine — the raft at Monte Carlo

'The Girls are making a flying visit to Monte Carlo!' It took them three days to get there via Dover, Calais, a train to Paris, and finally a coach to Monte Carlo. At a subsequent season they were less keen when they found they were expected to work on a raft near the famous Sporting Club. Eventually they became accustomed to the short trip to it by speedboat, the audience watching them from the casino.

Tiller's style of precision dancing was naturally admired in Germany. The outrageous May Sharples was in charge of the Girls there. She had graduated from dancing to small parts at the Winter Gardens but because there was difficulty in getting money out of certain managements in Berlin, she was now a non-dancing Captain. Frances Lunn describes her:

By the time I knew her, she was a mature woman. She'd got a big bust. She was notorious for having lots of love affairs which she told us all about. She'd been to South Africa and showed us some lovely diamonds. She tacked on to me because I was useful. I was good at sewing, you see, and a good knitter. She had me altering corsets. I sat there sewing instead of rehearsing which I needed.

The novel life abroad made Frances disenchanted with Britain when she returned home for a spell:

We got used to the lovely coffee and rolls for breakfast. There is no imagination here in England. Tea is very insipid after good coffee. We got used to having it with cream on the top, it was so thick. Underneath it was piping hot. In Vienna we had wiener schnitzel, beer and champagne. We couldn't understand it when we got back home, our mothers cooking us eggs and bacon.

Frances not only developed a love for foreign food but an obsession for flying:

When I first went up, I had to sign a paper to say it was my responsibility if anything happened. I was wrapped up in an officer's uniform; you couldn't see me for fur and leather. The pilot sat in front so I was in the back on my own. It was all in the open in those days. We went over the Alps. We landed and a meal was set out and after our picnic, we went off again.

The Mangon Tillerettes with an unexplained child

When she arrived at the theatre that night she saw a note pinned up at the stage door stating that it had come to the management's notice that a Girl had been flying, which was forbidden! There was no way she could get round the Captain now despite her talent for sewing.

With such exhilarating times, they found the Blackpool boys very ordinary on their return. It was an impossible transition for many of them to make after years of travel. Abroad they were fêted, courted like film stars but always in the security of a group; then when they went back home they were expected to slip from their previous lifestyles into houses that sometimes had no hot water or inside w.c. How could a working boy understand how a police escort had to be summoned in South America because there was such a large mob shouting and cheering for the 'Ingleses', or appreciate an imitation of Josephine Baker? Their relations and old schoolfriends would tell them they had stepped out of their class, which in fact they had. Some considered marrying their foreign boy-friends but hesitated:

It's a difficult decision but I knew if I married out there, well, there is a certain loneliness, yet going back to English life is unsatisfactory. I knew an English woman who married in Sweden. She had everything I wanted. A beautiful home, it was lovely but she was so homesick, she would cry when she thought of London. She had two children who only spoke Swedish, and she found she couldn't learn the language. I was glad I knew her because I realized what would happen to me.

Many of course did marry and stay abroad. Madame Derval, wife of the manager of the Folies, was Amy Campton, an early Tiller Girl. Another became Countess Pierbalancourt. But having courted and won a vivacious dancer the men usually wanted them to change:

When I got married, he wouldn't let me go to visit the Girls' Club. I think he thought it was a brothel. The French are so different. I used to ask what I should do to fill the day and he'd simply say go to the park and knit. We just had nothing in common and I couldn't communicate with his dull business friends.

Quite a few mothers nipped their daughters' dancing careers in the bud. The very same women who had been all for their daughters travelling abroad seemed suddenly to get bored with the idea. Perhaps it was because the glamorous life was too far away to show off their child to friends and relatives. Perhaps they just became jealous. Whatever the reason, the mothers often told their daughters that they should come home and look after them. It was a common attitude:

After I left Tillers, I just came home and looked after my mother. She wasn't terribly ill. Why should I have to come home? I had two sisters there already.

Poor Val Bryan never even managed to work abroad:

I worked in England but I always seemed to miss the good jobs abroad; every time I started rehearsing for something special, my mother would drag me away. She seemed annoyed I was lucky. Then when I was chosen with four others to go to the Folies, we were all excited about going then. Jennie called me into the office and said that I couldn't go as she had received a letter from my mother.

Maybe the mothers were fearful that their daughters would marry and live abroad, the idea of permanent separation being too painful. The answers will never be known as there were no confrontations. The 1920s girl did as she was told and came home.

After two or three years of utter boredom in the bosom of their family, marriage seemed the only answer to those forced back home. Many married shopkeepers and with typical Tiller discipline, enthusiasm and loyalty, they threw their energies into building good businesses with their husbands. Years later friendship is their strongest memory:

We never had the chance to feel lonely. We worked so hard together, chatted about our boyfriends, even shared our clothes. We looked forward to going to the theatre every evening. There was always something to talk about in the dressing-room.

If any wonder whether they made the right decision to come home and marry a British man, Dolly Howard who danced round the world had the wittiest appreciation of the difference between the continental men and the boys back home:

I went into the dressing-room and had to change with these men. You can tell what men were like over there, they never bothered when they got changed. I saw them putting on pale blue underpants. I thought, That's funny, I've never seen pale blue underwear before. Foreigners, they don't bother what they show.

6

'We Were the Cream de la Crême'

Going to America

WHEN WE first got to New York, the reporters met the boat and because they printed our names in the papers the Stage Door Johnnies started pestering us; they were a completely different sort from the European ones. Bolder. They would ring up and say, 'I'm your uncle!' I knew very well I'd not got an uncle in America.

What caused the men to be so desperate to contact the Girls? John's strict paternalism fascinated the New York newsmen who described it as 'Tiller's puritanical blue laws'. The *New York Herald* headlined 'These Girl's Don't Drink, Smoke or Flirt' and printed an article, attributed to Mary, in which she explained how difficult it was for her to maintain discipline in a society where young girls were surrounded on every side by such bad examples of free and easy ways in all walks of life. She claimed, and this certainly constituted a challenge to the American male:

No Tiller is ever seen with a man, she does not go out with a man, receive any man and the rule extends even to her father and brothers, no Girl holds a conversation with a man, inside or outside the theatre and if a man addresses her, she would say 'Excuse me' and walk away.

She quoted from an address that John was supposed to give to his troupes whenever they were about to tour:

I now expect you young girls to keep bright and shining. John Tiller expects each of his pupils to do her duty in keeping the Tiller standard flying high and white.

She reckoned that at this point, quite a few of them shed tears, but contrary to expectations there was apparently no Tiller flag hoisted or hymn sung. The article went on to announce that although 35,000 had passed through the Tiller schools, not one Girl had been involved in a divorce, they had nearly all got married and to keep the record straight she hastily added, 'Those that hadn't, all hoped to do so'.

Impressive reading it may have been for some, but tantalizing for the men and they certainly rose to the occasion. Apart from receiving numerous phone calls, the Girls learnt about the male New Yorker's favourite pastime, the chase. While window-shopping in Manhattan or on Broadway, they would find that they were being followed block after block, then, having sized up her figure and made certain the Girl was aware she was being followed, the man would walk ahead, glance round to check that her face was as good as her body and start a conversation. Whether successful or not, the hunter would make a charming farewell and stroll off to make another conquest. Often a second man would be standing by to perform the same ritual. Some of the Girls enjoyed such encounters; others loathed them:

They were that cheeky. In cafés they would come up and sit at your table and chat as though they had known you all their lives. I didn't like that at all.

Those that hated the familiarity rarely went out and left the States as soon as their initial contract was completed. Others went on dates and often married their suitors. Despite publicity about their strict code of conduct, it was obvious that the rules had been broken because when the time came for the first troupe to go home, John was astounded to learn that eight out of the sixteen had married during the run and intended to remain behind and every one of the other eight was engaged. In order to protect his investment in their training, he immediately inserted a clause into later contracts stipulating that no marriages take place during the booking. Naturally this was publicized in the newspapers.

At the height of their popularity in New York, there were three lines working in Broadway. As the *Lollipops* were finishing and preparing to go on tour, twenty-four Tiller Girls were in the *Ziegfeld Follies* and there were sixteen *Sunshine Girls* at the Globe Theatre. Although reporters gave the impression that the troupes were new to the American stage, they had in fact made their début as far back as 1900 when George Lederer booked them to perform their original *Pony Trot*. More recently Charles Dillingham and George White had visited the Palace Theatre, London, and were so impressed that they booked the Girls to appear in *Good Morning Dearie, George White's Scandals* of 1923, the *Nifties* of 1923 as well as all the Fred Stone promotions. The great Florenz Ziegfeld saw the forty-eight Girls in the Folies-Bergère in Paris and took them under contract for a six month spell into his own *Follies* which he extended to three years.

Mary Read, who had first worked in New York in 1916 with the *Sunshine Girls,* endeared herself to reporters by telling them of her great love of the city. She persuaded John to open a school at 226 West 72nd Street which incorporated an office where negotiations to import Tillers could be conducted, and a rehearsal studio where she trained American pupils as well as the troupes. She was a hard taskmaster but a considerably fairer one than la Belle Ethel. Objective rather than objectionable was the unanimous verdict of the proletariat who always addressed her as Miss Read. As soon as she gave up dancing in the line to supervise the school, her nubile appearance became plump as she enjoyed dining well, a

RKO studio shot showing Mary in charge

pleasure shared with John where the plumpness developed into fatness. When Jennie did finally cross the Atlantic in 1925, a rare photograph of the two women together shows them looking remarkably like Tweedledum and Tweedledee.

John was as diplomatic as Mary when talking to the press. When asked why the British Girls were so superior in his style of dancing he replied:

There are no girls on earth that have the beauty of face of the American girl, nor the peculiar charm of your lasses. But I doubt if American girls have the perseverence required to compete with Tiller Girls in dance and drilling. Of course America produces wonderful dancers, great soloists as the term goes.

By tactfully praising and criticizing at the same time, he had pupils flocking into the school, eager to train, rightly believing he had special abilities in this sphere. But he never put an American girl into one of his troupes.

Ethel, with her good looks, height and dancing standards, was naturally one of the first to be sent across. Finding that Mary Read was totally in control of all work out there, she swiftly gave in her notice. She had the sense to realize there could not be two Queen Bees within one organization, even in such a large country, and anyway it meant being separated from her lover Mangon.

The sea voyage from Britain necessitated daily rehearsals to keep the Girls limbered. These were usually called early in the morning to ensure that the other passengers were not disturbed. The Girls were highly embarrassed though when John transported two Pekinese dogs as a gift for Mary. Jennie always had two of the same breed yapping away in her office. She made it plain to them that she was upset by his tactless gesture.

After disembarkation, the first appointment was always with the furriers:

Whether we wanted to or not, we had to have a fur coat. I remember we arrived during a heat wave and had to go into this refrigerator where they kept the furs. We had to buy one; it certainly wasn't given and don't forget we hadn't been paid a salary while travelling. My friend had a leopard skin and I had a coney seal with a mink marmot collar and cuffs. Years later my mother could hardly wait for me to pass it on to her. It went all through the family. After the furriers we all trooped off to the same dentist who X-rayed our teeth which was unusual in Britain then.

Apartments had been booked for them in one block and they shared in couples. Most enjoyed the luxury of employing a cleaner to do their housework but a few took a puritanical delight in doing their own.

The wholesomeness of the Tiller Girls appealed to Fred Stone

It was theatre practice to put dancers in dressing-rooms situated at the top of the building which was totally illogical as troupes always had more changes of costume than solo acts and less time to complete them. On Broadway they appreciated the benefits of the most modern theatres in the world. Although still on the top floor, they now had lifts, or rather elevators, to take them up and once inside the dressing-room each Girl had her own mirror well lit by bulbs surrounding three sides just as they had seen in the films. Instead of tripping over their shoes while doing quick changes, each chair had pockets where they could thrust them out of the way.

In theatres all over the world performers are expected to turn up at the 'half' to start making up. In New York they were called an hour before the show opened, and once they had done their face make-up, they only had to put on tights rather than spend a long time carefully using wet white, which gave them longer to gossip. There were no restrictions about hair length as wigs were worn for most numbers.

Fred Stone was a Broadway star who used Tiller lines in all his shows at the Globe Theatre; *Tip Top*, *Stepping Stones*, *Criss Cross* and *Ripples*. His wife and daughter starred with him so the wholesomeness of the Tillers suited the family image he was anxious to present. One Head Girl had to reprimand an avid garlic eater. Unfortunately she had been placed next to Dorothy, Fred's daughter, in one routine. She complained to her father, he in turn to the Head Girl.

Life-size photographs were displayed outside the theatre during final rehearsals and an enormous amount of publicity was generated before the show but Opening nights always took them by surprise. American

Life had a feeling of unreality about it – as though they were acting in a film

audiences showed their appreciation as only they could. The applause that greeted them was like a thunder clap and went on for so long that the Girls could not hear the music and had to count under their breath to synchronize their kicks.

After the production had opened rehearsals were held only once a week; it was a comparatively easy life after the work in ciné-variety that most of them had done. After the show they would stroll back to their apartments and on the way visit the drugstores for a sarsaparilla or an ice cream soda. Life had a feeling of unreality about it, as though they were acting in a film all the time:

I was always broke. Very often I dined on a banana split, which was enormous: it consisted of a whole banana, three scoops of ice cream, syrup and whipped cream and only cost 25 cents; we also lived on delicatessen sandwiches and salads and were so excited with the automats where we put our money in and out popped coffee. No wonder I had a fat face.

Their salaries in America were usually $45 a week, the equivalent of £10. Income tax was minimal; Marie Webster had an old demand showing that of a total of $604 only $3.90 was payable. Through the Tiller office some lucky Girls received offers to advertise products. Two promoted silk stockings and Florence Stack appeared in newspaper advertisements praising Tokalon beauty products.

Florence Stack advertising Tokalon

TILLER'S GIRLS

Although most Tillers were spendthrifts and never had a ha'penny or cent to their names, Florence was a financial wizard. She loaned them money, saved it for them or doled it out when necessary, all the transactions being written on the souvenir programme of whatever show she was appearing in. The others said:

> Where there was money, there she was. She always had a sugar daddy. She was the best dressed Girl in the line. She even invested money in South Africa, listened and learnt what these men had to say. We couldn't understand a blind thing when she tried to explain to us.

Many of the shows were successful and there were many invitations to parties. They were thrilled when they suddenly realized that not only had Tom Mix and Gloria Swanson been in the audience on opening night but were in the same room with them at the party afterwards. Despite Mary's claim in the press, they were allowed more freedom in New York than ever before with their own apartments and telephones. There were certainly no more crocodile files or strictly supervised hostels.

New York is renowned for its effect on the personalities of outsiders and the Girls all went through a metamorphosis. Because there was no language barrier, everything seemed the same yet it was so very different. Their strengths and weaknesses were highlighted. The shy, quiet ones withdrew even more and had no wish to prolong their contracts. Yet when they did get home their families remarked how much more outgoing they had become. Others could not wait to merge into the New World and when marriage seemed to an easy route, they were soon sporting engagement rings off-stage but definitely not when Mary was around.

Rarely did any Tiller Girl stand out in a glamorous way but stunning was always the word used to describe Violet Bryant nicknamed Ginger because of her glorious red hair, she could not possibly blend in with the others. Those dancing next to her in the line always felt dowdy by comparison. With her hooded eyes loaded with mascara she was often likened to Myrna Loy and was eventually given a film test, a frequent occurrence for beauties in the 1920s. Nothing came of it as unfortunately she was not photogenic. When a famous cartoonist wrote asking if he could draw her she had no hesitation in accepting. With an unusual daring for a Tiller she took on the life of a Broadway dancer, the men flocked to her and she basked in their admiration.

In May the Girls would sit out on the steel fire escapes during shows and write home complaining about the unaccustomed heat. Because New York in the summer was too hot even for the natives, shows would close for a couple of months when the Girls would be sent home for a holiday on half pay, which was better than the average salary in Britain. After a few days swanking round relatives and old schoolfriends, the novelty of showing off the new clothes and slang such as 'She stinks on ice, kid,' wore off. The slower pace bored and irritated them so much that they longed to go back and their parents were almost glad to see them off.

When the Broadway productions finished, sometimes entire shows would go on tour. It was a grand chance to see all the states and sometimes Canada, even if it was rather too fast moving. The *Lollipop* timetable of

98

one night stands meant that they visited seventy-two venues in twelve weeks; although they did not venture further than St. Louis, it was exhausting and afterwards they could remember very little about each town. A comparatively leisurely schedule of *Yours Truly* still entailed travelling to twenty-one cities in thirty-five weeks. On this particular tour they were based in Chicago for seven weeks and expected to see gangsters shooting on the sidewalks every minute. This they avoided as they followed their Head Girl's strict instructions to keep out of the rough areas. They were astonished to find club owners using the city's violent reputation as a tourist attraction. One man made a point of showing the Girls the bullet holes in the walls and in their tablecloth. Another indicated the back of a diner and told them it was Al Capone. Mary would have had a blue fit if she had known about Ethel Ramsden's adventure:

> It was Prohibition times so I used to go to speakeasies. You'd knock on the door and a little slit would open. You never knew what you were drinking. We went to a place that was called 'Judges'. There were two black entertainers banging away at a piano. This owner called Judge, he got hold of me, promised me a motor car, a fur coat and I don't know what. I was so green I didn't know what was behind it and boasted that I could become Judge's Baby when I got back to the dressing-room. Of course the Captain forbade me to go anywhere near the place again.

The most remarkable booking was made in 1924 when Florenz Ziegfeld chose a troupe from both John and Lawrence to be in his *Follies* in New York. When the Lawrence Girls arrived, John's tended to be considerably older, having had to work their way up through their hierachy before being allowed into the promised land of show business. Taking a patronizing look at the newcomers, all aged only between seventeen and twenty and dressed in little check practice outfits, they decided that they looked childish and immediately nicknamed them the Tiller Babes.

The John Tillers were settled in the Ziegfeld Follies when the Lawrence Girls turned up in their practice outfits to join them. Considerably more sophisticated, John's Girls swiftly nicknamed the newcomers the Tiller Babes. The man in the dramatic pose is Herr Gross

Not only did Amy always travel with them but John was regularly at rehearsals. Fortunately the two groups only met at one session. John roared, 'Get that leg up' and struck his cane on the floor with an enormous bang. The Lawrence Girls froze with fear; their boss had often shouted but not with such force. Then they relaxed. John was chastising one of his own. All the same, they made sure they lifted their legs as high as possible. Apparently Ziegfeld spied on rehearsals by watching through a peephole in the wall.

Although there was very little difference between a 'John' and a 'Lawrence' in dance technique, their attitudes were totally different. John's firm having been established for nearly forty years by this time, the rival Lawrence Girls were definitely more earthy in character, with not a snob amongst them possibly because they did not have such a long tradition. At the time when both troupes were staying together at the English Girls' Club in Paris, although the Johns were convinced there was a rule that they should not mix, it never entered the others' heads. Free from outdated rules regarding outdoor clothing and morals, the Lawrences certainly had a more lively manner. Whereas a John Tiller never expected fairness, the Lawrences did and would speak out.

Although the Johns were shaken to the roots when the youngsters turned up, they avidly watched their routines. Having been brainwashed to think that all other troupes were inferior, they never ceased to be surprised when they managed to watch them dance. Even the perfectionists were impressed and admitted they came away with their tails between their legs having learnt a great lesson about false pride.

Marriage was forbidden in their contracts too, but so many of the so-called babes broke the rule during the season that Amy found it impossible to replace them; not having a large pool of dancers back in Britain she decided to bring the unmarried ones back after the first year's contract was completed.

The Girls black up for one of their routines

It suits managers, producers and directors to encourage naîvety in their dancers. That way, they query nothing and never answer back; as a result they are not known for their political judgement, but, during the Depression they were jolted into social awareness. They saw men trying to make money by selling apples and oranges at street corners and the brave attempt of others to look smart with well-polished shoes, pressed suits and hidden frayed cuffs. The obvious unfairness of such poverty side by side with conspicuous affluence reminded them of their vulnerable parents back home.

Mary Read continued to manage the school in New York after John's death. Completely independent, she took and needed no advice in theatrical matters; she had listened well to John, accepted responsibility and took every chance that came her way. She provided dancers for *Criss Cross, The Three Musketeers* in 1928 and *Ripples* in 1930. When the Girls left to get married at the end of each show, rather than risk Jennie's haphazard choice of replacements, she sent over the two Head Girls who were almost resident in America, Rene Todd or Dorothy Sabine, to make their own selection.

John was proved wrong in his observation that American girls did not have the perseverence to train to his standards of precision. After his death, the *Missouri Rockets* were formed. They evolved into the famous thirty-six *Rockettes* at Radio City Music Hall. Just as English dance directors eventually copied the Tiller style and undercut fees, so did the American managers. The union representing the performers were militantly opposed to British dancers taking work from them and there was a lean period for the sixteen Girls left.

Trying to live on a half salary of $25 was difficult. They moved to cheaper hotels where they were not supposed to have food in their rooms but took it in turns to get breakfast and hide tiny stoves in the wardrobes while waving the cooking fumes out of the window. They would go to restaurants for their main meal and take advantage of the generous portions served to share a meal between two. The ones able to secure 'sugar daddies' fooled the poor men into thinking that there was a Tiller rule that they only go out in twos and threes and so managed to get meals for their best friends as well. Banana splits still solved acute hunger problems but gorgeous undies were forgotten for the first time. Bravely they still tried to send a regular allowance home.

Their loyalty was rewarded when Mary signed a contract with RKO studios, initially for six months. It was real progress in the entertainment business. She negotiated a fee of $1,800 a week from which she had to pay the Girls' salaries of $45 each, netting considerably more for herself. They really were going to be in pictures. They were off to Hollywood!

Each member of the troupe had to sign the formidable contract. It was strictly binding concerning their exclusive services to RKO so there would be no perks for performing at parties or advertising products. As was to be expected in American contracts there was a paragraph prohibiting any act that would shock, insult or offend the community or degrade them in society.

One of the prettiest of this troupe was Bella Pilling; she was thrilled that her mother could buy the movie magazines that featured numerous

After John's death, Mary proved she had listened well by signing a profitable contract with the RKO studios

publicity shots of the troupe. Each time she finished a film, she would tell Mum the title and once it reached the cinema, Mrs Pilling was to be seen at every performance. Nicknamed Janet Gaynor by the make-up artists because of her resemblance to the star, she was generally liked not simply because of her sunny nature, but because she had a special hobby; she read the teacups. It was a quick route to popularity and she was invited out more than the others. When she was missing on the set, she could always be found in the stars' dressing-rooms. Bella never put on airs and graces, remaining a real Blackpool girl. The stars must have enjoyed her shouting out her catch phrase of ''old onto yer 'at' followed by her infectious laughter as she launched into their futures.

The Girls were most impressed when Mary bought a Daimler and employed a chauffeur so they in turn bought a car between them and shared the running costs. 'Tripping Tessie', as they called it, was the pride and joy of their lives. Richard Dix felt differently: 'Don't you put that tin thing next to my car,' he shouted as they parked. They were thrilled to meet members of the Kennedy family, Mary Pickford, Charlie Chaplin. Greta Garbo even asked to be introduced to *them*. She wanted to know if they liked America and appearing in movies. 'Just like a queen,' was their description of her manner.

All of them had been trained by the School from the age of eight or nine, eight having made their début at the Winter Gardens at Blackpool. After working in all the major cities on the Continent, they could allow themselves a little self praise. 'We were the cream de la crème,' recollects one.

102

At home in Manchester or
Blackpool parents were
thrilled to find numerous
publicity shots of their Girls
in movie magazines

For the few that returned to
Britain, life would never be
the same

While working in films Mary set the pattern of work for the next fifty years. She inaugurated the practice outfit that distinguished them in press photos — black pants, white blouse, ankle socks and the black bow tie that they were so nervous of mislaying. More important was the style of dancing which was now defined by a shorthand record of steps. They rarely performed as individuals; from now on they were to remain in line, arms linked behind each other. Despite their renewed popularity in the 1950s, no Tiller troupe had the pleasure of visiting America again.

They appeared with Irene Dunne in many films: *Three Cheers, Half Shot at Sunrise, Babes in Toyland* and so on. After the RKO contract expired the few unmarried Girls came home. Florence, the financial wizard, subsequently worked as a hostess in clubs in London. Bella married a butcher who displayed her photographs in his shop while she charmed the customers in the same way she had charmed the stars. As a final tribute to the American male, one Girl literally jumped ship as the gangplank was being pulled away, leaving her sister to face the music with their parents. And Ginger? Well, she was to dance for another twenty years.

Mary Read closed the school after providing one final line-up in the Princetown Follies in 1935. Then she married an American. In 1956 she visited Blackpool and the Head Girl at the Opera House was detailed to entertain her. She was never told by the London office or by Mary herself of the important part that Miss Read had played in the Tiller story.

7

'The Mrs Carries On'

The Lawrence Tiller Girls in the Folies Bergère Revue at the Victoria Palace

AFTER JOHN'S death in 1925 one New York newspaper ran an article describing how the Tiller business was progressing without the great man. The headline was 'The Mrs Carries On' and so she did. For many years, there had been no reason to scour the streets for pupils. Due to an unending stream of publicity in all manner of publications, there were constant applications by post and from dancers simply arriving at the office. To be a Tiller Girl was a golden vision. Newspaper publicity always gave the impression that the school could train anyone from scratch with little or no dance experience so young readers felt that they could just turn up without an appointment and would immediately be seen by this apparently motherly woman called Jennie Tiller. It was true; that was just the way it happened. The fact that she was such an eccentric character meant that only those with strong personalities survived. The audition of the Port twins was typical:

> I was climbing up all these stairs to the office and thought by the time I get to her, I'll be too puffed to dance properly. Knocked at the door and these Pekes starting yakking away. Mrs Tiller said, 'Take off your skirt, you can leave your hat on.' Good job I had a good pair of drawers on. I kept me beret on.
> I did two kicks, cartwheels and splits then she told me to get dressed.

I thought no way have I got in, it was too quick but she said I could start the following Monday.

Although they saw other Girls rehearsing in troupe, Elsie and Eddie Port seemed to be the only pupils who were training at the School. They laughed from morning to night:

We were taught by Jessie. Laugh, we never laughed so much in our lives. I always remember Jessie saying, 'Come on twins, let's go over the tap,' and we'd go through it to the tune *Sitting On Top Of The World*. When Jennie came in and asked to see what we were doing, we were giggling so much, she would say, 'What are yer giggling at, yer little monkeys?'

Elsie and Edith Port were so alike that Jennie dosed the wrong one with her cure for all ailments — castor oil. Here are the twins with their sister, Birdie

Jennie had other ideas apart from ordering 'See tha' gets tha's privates washed before tha' gets my costumes on.' She believed in building them up. She always paid for their meals during rehearsals and they would troop off to the Express Dairy cafeteria opposite. She stressed the importance of hot milk at night. For aches in limbs she would hand them Epsom salts. Next morning she simply would not accept they were still trembling all over but would just nod and say, 'Oh yes, I can see you're much better, luv.' She believed in the benefits of Turkish Baths for slimming. 'Oh Jessie, she's no good,' she would say in front of the poor, unfortunate Girl. 'Look at her knees, they're like piano legs, aren't they awful?' Then to the Girl, 'Yer legs are too fat, luv; go and have a Turkish Bath,' and hand her half a crown.

Sunny Rogers showed Jennie such deferential treatment that she was uncharacteristically taken aback:

Sunny Rogers (sixth from right) remembers Jennie going along the line pouring disinfectant on their bleeding feet

She was just going out of the door. I ran like mad to open it for her. 'What are yer doing that for? I'm not the Queen,' she said. I thought, all right, I'd better not do that again. Then when she was going out the next day and I made no attempt to open it, she said 'Where's yer manners?'

She rarely attempted to create new routines but one idea she did think up had painful consequences. She thought it would be clever for a team to kick 'on pointe' (on their toes). She knew they could kick well and seeing ballet dancers on pointe, not being a dancer, thought it would be simple to

Mangon Tillerettes

combine the two. She reasoned that if kicking dancers were so popular with audiences, the sight of kicking on pointe would astound them. She forced the Girls through their paces for a complete day, at the end of which they fell exhausted in a line on a bench. When they took their shoes off they found their feet were bleeding. Jennie summed up the problem in an instant and walked along the row pouring a bottle of disinfectant on their injuries, doubling their pain. Thankfully she did not persist in pursuing her mad idea.

Her methods of teaching were rudimentary, to say the least. Maisie Williams was thrilled when she was told to turn up the following week:

I thought I wonder what for? She never did tell people what they were going to be doing. When I got to the first rehearsal she announced, 'You're all going to be in the Command Performance.' Well I'd never been on stage in my life before and there I was, suddenly going to be in front of King George and Queen Mary.

I used to get so tired, she would hold up my black practice pants around the waist, hoist me up and down saying 'On yer balls, Girl, on yer balls.' I had to do extra rehearsals because I was new and she would daub my legs with methylated spirits and iodine. I used to go home on the train with striped legs. She was an absolute scream.

Her attempts to teach them a step was hysterical. She would mince about in her old fashioned winkle-picker shoes not knowing the first thing about dancing. 'Do this Girls, follow me.' Behind her back they were all doubling up with laughter wondering what she meant. 'Follow me, what are yer laughing at, yer daft things?'

As in all rehearsal studios there were large mirrors from ceiling to floor enabling the Girls to see their mistakes. Their bodies generated so much heat that the mirrors steamed up. Jennie did not realize the purpose of the mirrors and would shout, 'Don't be looking at yerself, don't be admiring yerself in the mirror.'

If the Girls were 'Tillerized' into thinking of nothing but the Tiller organization, so was Jennie. A line once appeared in Dublin in ciné-

variety. Afterwards the Head Girl reported back to her: 'It went very well, Mrs Tiller, better than *"Ben Hur!"* "Who's *Ben Hur*"?' she enquired, thinking it was a rival act.

When Francis Mangon was put in charge of the Rex Cinema in Paris, he presented the *Forty-eight Mangon Tillerettes*. The show was another ciné-variety bill, even better value than the British equivalent offering two feature films as well as variety. There were five shows a day, rehearsal starting sharp at 9 am, the show ending at midnight. One minute's lateness would earn a strict rebuke. They would even have to go through the new routines in between shows. There was a canteen for snacks in the building but they preferred to go to a bar in rue Pigalle where an Englishman, Fred Payne, would dish up their favourite meal which was still egg and chips.

The day before opening night was the time they all dreaded. The fact that Mangon fully deserved his title of Wizard of Lighting was of minor importance to the Girls who, due to his perfectionism, often only had a few hours' sleep in their dressing-rooms, and occasionally none at all. They were unable to appreciate the spectacle in the auditorium. Once seated the audience would see the theatre ceiling as though it were open to the sky at night; stars twinkling and a moon shining. A silver stairway on stage led down to the stalls. All Vera Manning knew was exhaustion:

We were dressed in net leotards covered with silver spangles, our gauntlets and berets too, from top to toe. There was a famous operetta star singing *Parlez-moi d'Amour*. We would start at the top of the stairs. Come down with a hand on each other's shoulders. By the time we were halfway down they were applauding like mad. When all forty-eight of us were on the stage, we couldn't kick in a straight line, so we danced in a semi-circle.

After we had rehearsed for three weeks, on the very last night of rehearsal, we worked till four in the morning then photos were taken of us in these spangled costumes; because they stretched from our ankles to our necks, we couldn't sit down. Two or three hours in these we were. In one shot I'm the only person not smiling, I was thinking 'sod this for a bloody laugh!'

At one point there were sixty Tiller Girls on stage dancing to *The Blue Danube,* all in blue picture hats with ribbons, midnight blue leotards and chiffon skirts. The orchestra was conducted by Oscar Straus. He was almost the most elegant man many of them had ever seen. Tall, slim, white-haired in perfect evening dress with the Star of Russia, an enormous ruby round his neck.

Mangon told them he had been unable to get work permits for a show at another venue. He asked, well told them, to double. So on top of the five shows and rehearsals every day at the Rex, they did another four at the Olympia and did not even receive double salaries but only one and a half.

The Rex/Olympia doubling soon finished but before they could relax to a comparatively simple régime of five shows a day, they were told to double at the Paramount. Off they went again, attempting to complete nine shows a day and remain sane. With greater experience they now organized themselves. The first one on stage had to be the first off the coach that trundled them to and fro. Over all this exhaustion Ethel Helliwell reigned supreme, supervising her 160 Girls. She frequently flew between Paris, Cannes, the Sporting Club at Monte Carlo and London for rehearsals. Thanks to her relationship with Mangon, she was well paid for her services:

> The secretary of the Mangon organization said, 'Your salary is ridiculous; as far as you're concerned, I'm going to see you get £10 for every theatre you work in.' So I made £70 a week. Then he looked after the income tax, which was a bit of a headache.

Her unique status had given her unusual confidence for a Tiller. By the 1930s she had stopped dancing in the line; there was hardly time in her schedule, but she and her sister Mabel would sometimes perform a fan dance duet in ciné-variety bills. 'Mabs', as she was affectionately called, also did a great deal of choreography. She had the same tall grace and was equally good looking in a gentler way with great soulful eyes. Although Mabel was a more sympathetic personality than her sister Ethel, when it came to discipline she was equally strict, the difference being that she did not take pleasure in enforcing the ruthless repetition that was necessary to get the routines to perfection and consequently the Girls adored her.

Nine shows a day plus rehearsals was too much for them. They were young enough to cope with the physical exhaustion but trying to memorize so many routines became unbearable. They were glad to be sent to Cannes to recuperate with only one show a night.

It was a great shock to the Girls when Jennie died on 21 February, 1936. Although she had been seen at the school less frequently over the past few years, rehearsals and contracts were organized so smoothly that the dancers had not noticed her gradual disappearance. Whereas John's will had been full of retribution, Jennie in one sentence thanked the thirteen people she considered important in her life and asked that they should simply 'share and share alike'. It was truly democratic; she not only named six Head Girls, Mr Smith and Miss Doris but had not forgotten the loyalty of William. She even charitably included Mary Read. In fact she was following her husband's wishes that those who had helped create a fortune should now inherit it.

The decline of the entertainment business generally was reflected in her estate. The houses in Blackpool, London and Manchester had been sold long ago. The company flats and rehearsal studios were on short leaseholds. The Tiller fortune had now dwindled to just over £3,000.

It was unlikely that anyone knowing Jennie would have agreed with the description of her occupation on the death certificate — widow of John Tiller. For all her strange behaviour in rehearsals and in the office, she had held her position as director for eleven years and during that time the Tiller troupes still commanded the highest respect and dominated all other dance troupes. Despite her eccentricity and the fact that they couldn't help laughing at her, the Girls would readily acknowledge that she gave them as much, if not more, affection than they had received from their own parents. Her belief in their abilities and the ideas she instilled into them had carried them through situations that they would otherwise have found impossible. The bond was so strong that they would feel her presence all their lives. She certainly did not live in the shadow of John; she was her own person and deserved to be described as more than a widow. Although they knew they would never forget Jennie, the Girls wanted her to have a permanent memorial so they had a collection and made a most practical and fitting choice: a marble floor for the church of St Stephen on the Cliffs, Blackpool.

After Jennie's death, William's life seemed to take a rapid downward course. He had become increasingly dirty and unkempt. Without any reason he left the Firm of his own free will and went to live in Brighton. He felt confident enough of the friendship of Doris and Mr Smith to visit them regularly but they felt distressed to see his appearance deteriorating so fast. Mr Smith started to give him new clothes but soon realized that William had no wish to be clean, as on the next visit the new suit would be filthy. Eventually he was taken into the West Sussex hospital and when Mr Smith visited him, he asked for some chlorodyne. A nurse intercepted him before he left and queried whether William had requested it. Apparently he had become addicted to it and the gradual disintegration of William was at last explained.

Now the full weight of responsibility fell on Doris. Mr Smith had firmly kept to his intention of dealing only with the financial side of the business and absolutely refused to participate in the selection of Girls. In many ways life was easier for both of them. They no longer had to wait for the elusive Jennie to finish making a steak and kidney pudding before sanctioning an important business decision, but they had taken over in lean times and Doris began to find the strain intolerable. For so many years, she had been tied morning, noon and night to Jennie. Now it was a solitary life.

There was general unemployment in the country which in turn affected the attendance of audiences so offers of work were dwindling. Lean times were getting leaner. In ciné-variety the mighty Wurlitzer replaced not only the orchestra but performers too. To top it all Mangon and Ethel had a row which unfortunately affected the employment of a large number of dancers. After years of blatant unfaithfulness, Mangon formed a serious relationship with a *soubrette* in the show. Although he had dallied with other performers, this time it was the final straw for Ethel — this one, she considered, was rotten at her job!

The atmosphere between them was chilly enough for the most naîve Girl to notice. One day he threw a book at Ethel in front of them. That was it; she stormed out, left Paris immediately, returned to Blackpool and married her childhood sweetheart. She never danced again and rarely attended a theatre.

As far as the Tiller office was concerned, the quarrel was acute and the consequence far reaching: they not only lost the services of Ethel but because Mangon stopped booking the Girls, all 160 jobs were lost. The combination of so many factors contributed to a serious decline in the contracts on offer. Quite a few Girls went into variety acts, sometimes forming their own. The less courageous ones sat in the Express Dairy café with all the other out-of-work performers. All through the week they gathered waiting for someone to pop his or her head round the entrance

While Edith is seated in a possessive position on his right, Mangon typically holds another Girl's hand

and shout that there was an audition, and they were off like a shot, their audition clothes naturally packed in a case by their table. Thursday was the highlight of the week. *The Stage* was published on that day and they would sit at tables in threes and fours sharing a single cup of coffee. Everyone was generous about sharing job information and they had the bonus of the Tiller name behind them. If they were on their beam-ends, the really desperate might brave an audition with the dreaded Sherman

The *Daily Mirror Eight* Girls

Fisher. Like many dance directors he imitated the Tiller style and by undercutting could offer some work.

No matter how long they had been unemployed, the Girls felt guilty when auditioning for other troupes. The ghost of Mrs Tiller would loom above them telling them they were letting her down.

An unusual job was created by a national newspaper for publicity purposes. A team called the *Daily Mirror Eight* toured seaside towns during the summer from June till the end of August. Doris and the editor auditioned dancers who had to perform physical exercises along with acrobatic dancing. They rehearsed at New Cross Stadium and had to get a suntan to look fit. Once they were on the road they had their own coach, staying a day or half a day in each town. It was free to the public, promoting the *Daily Mirror*. They performed in the park if there was one and on the sand if there was not. That proved difficult as they couldn't balance and the kicking routine was murder! The audiences particularly loved the Indian clubs routine and after the show would come up and rub their suntan to see if it was real. The Girls who got the contract loved it; they earned £8.10s a week and stayed in the best hotels. At each town the Captain had to greet the mayor and they tucked in to an excellent meal afterwards.

The Girls were aware that there was considerably less work available but did not realize that the finances of the school were causing serious concern. Francis Laidler was still using the troupes for his superbly lavish pantomimes. He had been a loyal supporter for many years, his business relationship stretching back to the 1900s when he booked John's touring pantomimes. Now he presented an average of five on his own, always booking the Girls. Considering that he started his adult life as a wine and spirits salesman, he had certainly learnt the art of showmanship: whatever the fluctuating state of the theatre, he always managed to pay an enormous wage bill for his large casts.

Emile Littler was a much younger producer of rival pantomimes; feeling more than a little disloyal, Mr Smith wrote to him in desperation suggesting that he might be interested in his dancers. Littler was a wily businessman who knew very well that things were difficult for them and realized how badly they needed his business. Although he had no doubts about the Girls' standard of work he would only take up on Smith's offer if his organization was efficient. He insisted that he should visit the Tiller office so that he could observe at first hand how things were run. A deal was made which was of great benefit to both sides as Littler went on to present pantomimes for many years, sometimes as many as a dozen annually. The fact that Laidler and Littler often had Tiller troupes in the same town without conflict said a great deal for the professional attitude of the producers concerned.

An outstanding Girl at this time was Phyl Blakeston. Unusually tall, even for the Plaza troupe which was her line, her excellent dancing seemed to come so naturally to her, that the other Girls were full of praise for her work.

Littler was attracted by her elegance and firm authority when she was Head Girl in one of his shows and he persuaded her to work in his organization and leave Tillers. She took the opportunity despite the fact that many of her colleagues let her know that they judged her disloyal. Phyl would have stayed in show business without the help of Littler but she was fortunate in that she met him at the right time, when he was building up his pantomime empire. Unlike with Mangon and Ethel there were no angry scenes for the Girls to witness. They had mutual respect and remained devoted friends till he died in 1985.

One of Phyl's Plaza chums, Mignon Harman had an unhappy life at this time; she had been adopted by a doctor and on the surface was a vivacious person spending her time playing cards and laughing with the rest of them. She was supposed to be engaged to a wealthy young Jewish boy whom no one ever met, and they began to wonder if he existed. She was unusually affected for a Tiller, wanting to be called Mignon Diamanté. Those outside the card-playing school viewed her suspiciously because she seemed to get embarrassing crushes on a few of her colleagues. The friendship between the Girls can aptly be described as sisterly. It was very undemanding, revolving round the borrowing of clothes, and helping each other with routines. For Mignon it often meant more and her co-workers realize, looking back with the wisdom of a long lifetime, that she wanted a lesbian relationship with more than one of them. Tragically she never chose anyone who cared to respond. She attempted suicide several times, always while working and in highly dramatic circumstances, starting with threats at the top of the Commodore, Hammersmith. Of course in such unenlightened days no one attempted to reason with her. It was well beyond the comprehension of most ordinary people, let alone the inhibited Miss Doris. After her third attempt she was sacked. Years later at the age of thirty-eight, she finally killed herself.

Life for Ginger had become a roller-coaster but she was a survivor. Like other Girls back from America, she continued to accept whatever job was offered. It must have been dull touring around Britain after Broadway but she knew of no alternative. Her real sweetheart was an alcoholic but although he was her one and only true love she had impetuously married a

The morale of the Lawrence Tiller Girls was high when they appeared in two Royal Command Performance shows before he retired in 1936

solicitor. Quickly realizing that the relationship would never work, there was a terrible row in which she threw the wedding ring at him and stormed out. Going back to her old love was impossible because of his drinking habits. When he finally died of alcoholism, she returned to the only job she knew, dancing. She was invaluable for remembering original routines, which she had learnt from old John Tiller himself. She was made Head Girl and although it was not acknowledged by anyone in authority, she was already drinking too much.

The dilemma of whether to marry was more coolly assessed now. Bandboys were fun but strictly barred by the Tiller office. The unusually benevolent Mr Smith had strong words to say about them:

> I never had a great respect for bandboys; they're all booze and troublesome. I never like them. They're all right individually I've no doubt.

Ethel of course had had her own way of dealing with their advances. When exiting from the stage, a first violinist bent down in fake adoration to kiss her feet. Without hesitation she kicked him under the chin, the full weight of the kick throwing him flat on the floor. In fact Mrs Hylton, in her turn, forbade her musicians to fraternize with the dancers, but at least two Girls married her boys.

Nowadays, Girls would deny that they had ever even conversed with a man working backstage. One Girl felt the full force of snobbery when she announced her wedding to a stagehand. Knowing the troupe's constant hunger, she arranged an enormous spread for the reception and was hurt when no one from her troupe turned up. The spiteful Head Girl had deliberately called a sudden rehearsal. At least she had the satisfaction of a long marriage to a devoted husband.

'All the Best', Opera House, Blackpool, 1938

After the free and easy theatre life, marriage to a staid man could present problems:

> My husband didn't like me talking about the theatre although he had encouraged me to do so when we were courting. He was a flight lieutenant. One of the lads asked me at a dance how I had earned my living before I had got married. 'Oh, I was a Pro,' I said. Well you could have heard a pin drop. Naturally I meant a 'Pro' in the theatre sense. My husband was furious, so was I. When I got home I said, 'They ought to know you better than think you would marry a prostitute.'

Unless a dancer was resident for many weeks at a theatre, it was difficult to get to know a prospective husband. The man had to have great financial resources and staying power to follow the Girl if she went on tour. A considerable amount of objectivity was necessary if a really wealthy man decided to sweep a Girl off her feet.

During the difficult times in the thirties, the bread and butter money for Tillers was made at Christmas through the patronage of Laidler and Littler so an offer of a regular summer season was eagerly accepted by the office. The wholesomeness of the Tiller dancers suited the Popplewell family who presented a variety show at the Gaiety Theatre, Ayr. At that time a new dance director had risen through the ranks. Her name was Barbara Aitken. As a fourteen-year-old she had made her début in a particularly sophisticated team, and went on to appear on Broadway. Suddenly in the thirties she announced that she was both too thin and too old to dance any more. Immediately Miss Doris decided to promote her to dance arranger. It was an obvious and necessary position which should have been filled long before. Since Ethel had left, no one had taken her place. Numbers had been revived but no Head Girl was allowed to create new ones. Ginger's character was too erratic to risk letting her have complete control so Barbara was the appropriate choice. Wisely she was given the Popplewell season. It was a simple enough brief and far enough away for mistakes not to be seen by West End producers.

When war was declared in September 1939 the Popplewells, like all other managements, closed their theatre immediately. But in the beautiful autumn of that year, there was a feeling of unreality. The country was at war and yet nothing seemed to be happening; everything looked so peaceful. So the theatres reopened. The Popplewells told Mr Smith that they would continue with the show but as the country was in such a state of uncertainty they would not be able to pay the Girls' wages! As he knew there would be no uncertainty about accepting the admission fees from the audience, he told them he would not accept and instead negotiated a nominal fee which at least kept the dancers in work. The show continued until Christmas by which time Mr Smith and Doris realized they were facing up to a new way of life that would challenge them even more than the lean and difficult times of the thirties.

8

'Will There Be Food?'

The end of a routine — and look at the relief!

THE WAR certainly altered the Girls' priorities. All thoughts of glamorous undies disappeared and an intense preoccupation with food took over. 'I've managed to get an onion, I'll post it to you,' wrote one mother. Another was equally proud to promise a Christmas pudding made with carrot. Most of the work on offer now involved touring so problems arose with the basics of life. Ration books were issued and as they trailed round looking for food, they would mutter 'Eyes and teeth, Girls' to each other and try to charm the shopkeepers into giving them something extra. Usually they were successful and for some reason butchers seemed particularly susceptible and they would almost waltz out of the shop with a specially good piece of meat.

One essential survival technique was to make room for a couple of packets of powdered egg in their suitcases as the real thing was so scarce.

At breakfast they would barter with each other over the large portion of margarine and the much smaller amount of butter allowed.

Food rationing tested their landladies' skill and disposition. A week of brilliantly created meals could easily be followed by boiled and chipped potatoes being served on the same plate every day for the next seven days.

Bad luck in picking inferior digs was courting disaster. Constant headaches through sheer lack of food were common:

> Nellie, one of the Terrys, collapsed in the fish and chip shop one night. Anaemia, the doctor said it was. Overwork. So they cut down on rehearsals for a while.

Anxious mothers sent whatever food and clothing they could lay their hands on. It was not unusual to receive a parcel with cakes and a jumper packed together.

Fortunately there were many invitations to parties so they were able to ward off starvation. The only query they ever raised before accepting was 'Will there be food?' Somehow their hosts miraculously rose to the occasion and provided a good table for the ever-ravenous dancers. Of course the Americans were able to outshine any British effort when they arranged social gatherings at their camps. Despite their reputation for being 'over-sexed, over-paid and over here', the lure of food was difficult to resist and the Girls would eagerly jump into the coach sent for them. Meryl Hughes was frank about her reason for going:

> I went simply because of the food. Usually it had been flown in. Huge heaps of steaks and hard boiled eggs were put along a counter-like table for us to help ourselves. I wasn't interested in smoking or talking to Americans. I would take my carrier bag, fill it and then sit waiting. I'd be wondering when we'd go home only five minutes after I'd arrived.
>
> I just didn't get on with them; I was a serious thinker. The first thing I wanted to know was their politics, and they didn't like that. 'Oh, come on sister, let's dance, let's smooch.' I hated that.

All round the country, theatre shows carried on through the air raids. First the sirens would wail a warning, then would come the announcement: 'Ladies and gentlemen, if you wish to leave the theatre, please do.' No one ever did and they became almost blasé even when the bombs dropped. True, they admit to having felt a little uneasy while up in the *Flying Ballet* at the Coliseum when some landed nearby, but the show went on as usual. If the all-clear had not been sounded by the time the finale was reached an impromptu concert was given by the cast, and if the raid continued after their improvisational skills were exhausted, members of the audience often took over. It was quite usual to stay in the theatre till two or three in the morning.

London was undoubtedly the worst hit of all the places they worked. When booked for the Hackney, Shepherds Bush and Finsbury Park Empire circuit during a particularly heavy phase, the raids continued on till morning and the Girls had to sleep in the theatre most nights. A week at Collins, Islington, was really dreaded. The dressing-rooms there, being in the basement, were regularly flooded and having to walk along a narrow plank for each costume change was not much fun. The management provided the minutest light imaginable so they bought candles as it was impossible to make up otherwise. To add to the squalor, rats ate the greasepaint sticks if they were left out.

When it was at last safe to leave the theatre, the Girls picked their way through pitch-black streets. Once inside the tube stations, they had to step over rows of people staking their claim to a space for the night. Some would be asleep already and women would be putting curlers in their hair or creaming their faces. Occasionally the Girls were forced to sleep there and the WVS women coming round early in the morning with a free cup of tea would see they were theatricals and demand a performance.

Of course there were narrow escapes which terrified their parents, such as the direct hit on a house next to the theatre during their performance and a theatre chandelier dropping on to the centre aisle just seconds after they had run that way. And there were many tragic scenes, including a baby being found in the rubble while the mother frantically scrabbled for its twin. A few Girls lost their entire families while working away from home but miraculously not one Tiller was killed while on contract.

Travelling to the next job was a major wartime problem. No matter how short the journey, rail travel always seemed to take up the entire day on Sunday as there were so many more missed connections then. At the inevitable change at Crewe, the first train would be late, and seeing their second one just pulling out, they would scramble to gather together personal luggage and company skips, shouting 'Hold the train', and screaming with laughter run along the platform and try to open a carriage door as the train was on the move.

For security reasons all railway stations had their names dimly lit so immediately dusk fell a strict count had to be kept of each one passed. Too much laughter instead of concentration led to many a group finding itself shunted into a siding for the night. The trains were crammed full and it seemed cruel to turf out soldiers from the carriages that had been reserved for their theatre companies. The young men would be packed like cattle in the corridors, sitting on their suitcases, and so tired that they were dropping asleep.

All men aged between nineteen and forty were called up for military service so the ones allowed to perform were considerably older than the dancers. Preferring to drink amongst themselves or start up a card game at every possible moment, they bored the Girls to tears.

The Girls' regulation practice outfit consisting of black pants, bow tie and white blouse was a useful alternative when skips of stage clothes went missing en route. Footwear proved an insurmountable problem, however. The Tiller office could not manage to provide new shoes for every production because clothing was as strictly rationed as food. A single skip which held the total stock of shoes was in the office stuck between Mr Smith and Doris at their desks; it was up to the Girls themselves to find a pair that fitted.

Hot black was still used by the old-timers but the younger set now spat into mascara blocks. A few adventurous ones, desperate for a more dramatic effect, tried other tricks. Black paper was cut into the thinnest fringe possible and stuck onto their eyelids. This seemd the ultimate in glamour as they fluttered their eyes across the stage at each other. Sonia Hurst Thompson, who had made her stage début in *Madame Beeton's Orange Pippins,* had a more effective idea. She cut a piece of her hair, rolled it round a matchstick, snipped it along the middle and laid the tiny fringe onto a slim strip of sticky plaster. Within days of her joining any

118

Bare legs, but wet white does
the trick

show the whole troupe would be displaying her efforts on their eyes.

Life could certainly be described as sticky if the Head Girl was not accurate with her measurements while making up the wet white. Stinginess with the glycerine made the legs sting and too much made them stick together! Tights were so expensive that they were not worn in many shows; the overall effect was no better anyway. Once wet white had dried on the legs, a lovely sheen could be got by rubbing the hands over it. The Girls actually preferred using it as the seams on the tights of the time were terribly coarse and felt like a thick ridge underfoot; standing or dancing in them for hours on end became unbearable.

Within months of war being declared women's clothes became more practical and austere. Boiler suits and slacks were popular; in those the Girls could cope with anything that might happen in an air raid, but they did make every effort to look as glamorous as possible off-stage. Because clothes were in such short supply, they happily lent or swopped outfits.

Life was slowed down by the time taken to queue for the necessities of life. If, say, a clothing book was lost, it took nearly two hours to collect a replacement. For Joyce Lee obtaining a smart pair of shoes was worth recording in her diary:

We were up at 7.15 am to get some cocktail shoes, toeless and heelless wedges, very smart they were. There was a terrible queue at 8.30. By the time we got served at 8.45 they had sold them all so instead I managed to get some court shoes; for £2.15s and seven clothing coupons. Mum and Brian lined up too; they were still queueing when I left at 10.20. We all felt very tired for the rest of the day.

119

Joyce was lucky: it was common to find fifty women in any queue for shoes and there was a near riot when 100 pairs of wedge-heeled shoes were delivered to a shop in Edinburgh.

Lives were brightened at six and ten past eight every evening. It was House Full for every performance and the audience response was exceptional. Tiller routines had always been well received but now audiences generated such warmth back to the performers that the Girls felt intoxicated at the end of the evening.

Most theatre managers did their utmost to be kind to them; even the parsimonious Littler paid for drinks all round on the first night, which impressed the newcomers.

His rival Laidler, however, being a thoroughly down-to-earth Yorkshireman, really understood their priorities when he announced to the company that, as butter had gone up, they'd all be getting half a crown more. Somehow he was still managing to produce pantomimes up to his lavish standards. Three troupes appeared in every production: the famous *Sunbeams,* who were his own juveniles and trained by the ex-Tiller Zeiky, a team of *Tillers*, and also a line of local girls. This made a total of thirty-six as well as a dozen principals in each company and still he offered to give them half a crown extra.

Somehow Laidler still presented 36 dancers, flying ballets and waterfalls in all his pantomimes during the war years

There was hostility between the two sets of adult dancers. This was generated by the fact that the Head Girls told their charges not to fraternize with the mill girls, as they called the locals. Not surprisingly the latter thought the Tillers arrogant.

A typical war-time troupe. Tiller Girls have the small neat bowties, the local Girls made their own

Some of the local girls really were millhands and the reason for their lack of dancing skill was simply that there were very few teachers available. Laidler did not appreciate the difficulty facing the Tiller Head Girl when production numbers had to be drummed into heads that were not used to picking up steps quickly. Wynne Lacey sat in the stalls with Laidler during one rehearsal and watched a complete fiasco on stage:

I remember I'd arranged a ballet and he wanted them all on points. He'd already given them pointe shoes and as he watched he complained that they were not on their toes. I just exploded. 'Mr Laidler, they can hardly walk properly, let alone get on their toes. I can't make them ballerinas overnight.' I really went for him and he climbed down. I felt lucky because normally he wouldn't accept anyone else's point of view or advice.

The abrupt way in which productions were disbanded affected Tillers. Frequently a show would be cancelled even before the first rehearsal when theatres were bombed, and all concerned would be forced to re-organize their lives at a moment's notice. Working in show business always led to an erratic life but now performers were pushed to their limits physically and financially. Of course they were grateful to Laidler and Littler for a considerable amount of work at Christmas time. In turn Littler was so proud when he was given a silver cigarette box inscribed 'from 1,000 Tillers'. Year after year the two producers presented pantomimes that were immensely popular. Immediately their box offices announced that panto bookings were open, queues formed round the block with people prepared to wait hours for tickets. By the first night, the entire season was usually sold out and new dancers, not realizing the situation, had to persuade the theatre fireman to let their relatives stand at the back of the auditorium. Everyone, managers and artists alike, could manage to pay their bills and even save a little by Easter as by audience demand these pantos usually ran from Christmas Eve until April. One record breaking production continued until May.

Different styles of dancing were popular

After a long season in pantomime, the Girls were fortunate if they got summer season contracts as they would run for an average of twenty weeks. Due to the lack of male stars around, many shows tended to be of the concert party type. The Girls liked these because they were booked in sets of only four or six dancers. Since John's death in 1925 any chance of principal roles had disappeared and they felt that being in a quartet gave them a chance to shine. These shows had a weekly change of programme. Rarely was a dance repeated during the twenty-odd weeks, which meant that an incredible number of routines had to be created and learnt. Rehearsals lasted throughout the season and every known style of dancing was used. Now at last, the balletomanes and tap fanatics were able to distinguish themselves instead of simply kicking in a line.

The stress of wartime did seem to unite people. There certainly were more approachable principals around. Life was fun with Cyril Fletcher, Dickie Murdoch and others. Two of the most generous who led touring companies were Norman Evans and Albert Modley. Both would hire coaches and take the entire company out to the country, arrange and pay for tea for them and then after a glorious day of laughter, the entire busload would sing all the way back to the theatre to do the show. The stars' generosity was deeply appreciated as the weeks led into months and months of monotonous touring.

Modley was outrageous, full of tricks on the Girls, popping large pieces of homemade toffee into their mouths just before they went on, or he would undo the zips at the back of their costumes while they were standing in line on the stage waiting for the curtain to go up. Unlike the cruel Crazy Gang in later years, he had no wish to embarrass them while they were performing so he would swiftly zip them up again just in time for the curtain to rise.

On one tour, the musical director and the Head Girl did not get on at all well. This was not unusual as that particular relationship usually seemed to be dogged by animosity, but one night this conductor went too far.

Bunty Gordon, the daughter of Harry Gordon, who had become a Tiller Girl, described the incident:

He really was the most peculiar man I'd ever met in my life. This night he must have been drunk, mad or both. The music was *Poet and Peasant*; he conducted it faster and faster. The fact that we managed to keep up with the music seemed to make him more furious, he became almost demented and went even faster.

Dear old Albert Modley heard the music from his dressing-room and shot down to the side of the stage. 'Eh, what the bloody 'ell is 'e doing to the Girls', I heard him say in the wings.

The audience was utterly bewildered trying to follow our legs, it was like a speeded-up film. Modley had his spot immediately we had finished. He strode to the front of the stage and said to the audience, 'Well, as you can see, the Tiller Girls have been working double time. I don't know what that lad is doing down there but, bloody 'ell they've been working 'ard.'

Of course not all the stars were as charming as Modley and Evans. There was the famous illusionist who was absolutely loathed, and unfortunately the Tiller office accepted several tours with him. He was a dour individual who screamed with rage at his assistants whenever anything went wrong with his act. Because he had such a foul temper there was a rapid turnover of assistants so often the smallest Tiller would be summoned to take over for a while. Their part in the act involved very little effort, just getting into a box before the start of the act, squeezing onto a tiny ledge which was curtained off from the audience and remaining there till the end of his act. They hated doing it. They were petrified of making a mistake and receiving a barrage of shouting. In addition, as his act was long, they resented missing the fun in the dressing-room and the fact that they were not getting extra pay.

They were delighted when his conceit took a public bashing at Crewe station. The train was well overdue and the platform packed with people. His wife's attitude to the station staff was embarrassing: 'You really shouldn't keep the great man waiting,' she repeated to all and sundry. Suddenly he opened his case, took out his wand, went to the edge of the platform and flourishing it said dramatically and loudly, 'Train arrive!'

Then he put the wand away, stepped back and stood waiting with his arms folded. Just as he did in his act. Sure enough, the train drew in immediately. He picked up the case, expecting to get a carriage. But as the engine reached them, they realised it had no carriages and it sailed straight past. His face was a picture, he could not believe his magic had not worked. He strode off in a fury while everyone on the platform roared with laughter.

There certainly was more seediness surrounding them on tour. Drink was the cause of many funny incidents. In one pantomime the Goose fell downstairs in a stupor, broke her leg and had to be taken to hospital with her costume still on. In another, two of the *Terry* juveniles got drunk and their matron frantically tried to sober them up between scenes by putting their hands under cold water. At the Lyceum, a witch who was supposed to fly across the stage missed her landing point. Below her, the Girls tried to carry on dancing, crying with laughter as she flew backwards and forwards several times until she made it. One Wardrobe Mistress was too heavy with the starch as she ironed their frilly knickers, so that for two complete performances, until the knickers could be washed and dried, they found themselves walking and dancing with their legs apart.

Despite the war, the Girls' standards were still high. They got better money and dates than other troupes and thanks to the dictates of Miss Doris, they had more pride in their appearance. Looking around at the tiredness of the servicemen and civilians, they were grateful to be in a job they enjoyed. However, all wartime contracts were subject to immediate cancellation if the theatre was closed and they were of course liable to be called up. Most dreamed of getting into ENSA rather than work in factories but so did Pros with fully rehearsed acts. ENSA would only book an act if everyone in it had been called up. Josephine Levy, who did get into ENSA, was disappointed:

> We thought we were going to bring culture to the boys. We got a nice couple of routines arranged to classical music. When we arrived, we were told to dance on top of two tables so that everyone could see us. As they hadn't seen a woman for months, we soon realized by their remarks it wasn't our dancing they were admiring.

Due to conscription there were only very young or comparatively old dancers around. The new recruits seemed giants to little Wynne Lacey. They towered over her as she tried to knock them into shape.

> Most of the ones I had to teach were huge. I swear they were beginning to get big on the free orange juice, milk and cod liver oil given out. Something was happening. God, they were big and so terribly young.

The oldest of them all was undoubtedly Ginger. She felt embarrassed still to be dancing in the line with Girls young enough to be her daughter whereas Barbara, her contemporary colleague, had at least become a choreographer. Ginger's hair was still a glorious red and people now compared her to Rita Hayworth. It was rumoured that famous artists had painted her but the keen-eyed youngsters noticed that her face was quite wrinkled. Audiences were unaware of this at a distance as she still had her wonderful bone structure but it was unfair that her skin should age prematurely and she dreaded anyone knowing exactly how old she was. When one dancer excitedly mentioned her twenty-first birthday, she warned her not to admit to it: 'If you do, they'll never let you forget it.' Then during one traumatic evening, she had an upsetting reunion with an old friend. The ex-Tiller visited the dressing-room and proudly boasting that they had worked together, she produced a scrapbook of photographs. The girls all crowded round to see it. The style of outdoor clothes immediately gave the era away. 'Good God, what year was that?' they asked. It was the twenties. Ginger was noticeably distressed but everyone was intrigued and persisted in trying to persuade her to share her memories. Ginger was determined not to be embarrassed a second time when another old friend visited her. But the friend recalls:

We were such good pals. I thought of her as a sister. We had lived together, I wrote letters for her, washed her hair. I was so excited that I was going to see her again. Took special care in choosing my clothes, just like a first date! I went back stage and she came downstairs in costume. All she said was 'Hello, kid' and walked past. It was such a let down. When you've left a show, they cut you dead.

Despite the passing years there was a stream of affluent men meeting Ginger at the stage door every night. She would make a grand appearance in her film star glad rags, fox fur capes and expensive perfume. The shy Girls envied the way she still could attract a wide circle of men but she simply went out with them as a meal ticket. During the last two years of the war she became more and more bitter. As a Head Girl she was a definite liability, turning vicious when she had too much to drink.

Neither Doris nor Barbara knew how to deal with the situation; they felt unable to issue an ultimatum, although they would have been justified. With the rest of the dancers they were like two headmistresses setting the tone of a select girls' school which grew more restrictive as the years went by. When choosing dancers John Tiller's criterion of a pretty face and smile was disregarded; they used the solo audition to judge the applicant's character as much as her dancing ability. It was a certain type of personality they were after. Only if she appeared hardworking, sedate and submissive would she be taken on. John's wish that the Tiller standard should be 'kept flying high and white' became their obsession.

Doris was nevertheless warm and approachable; everyone felt they could go to her with any problem, and they did. She also inspired loyalty:

If Miss Doris had said we should cut our throats, I really think we would have. She had that effect on people. I never once saw her lose her temper. If she had to rebuke someone, she would do so with such sweetness and motherly charm, you would feel knee high to a mouse.

In all her letters to past and present Girls, she finished with a delightful

125

personal touch by signing 'Mee' and a small drawing of a happy face beside it.

Reaction to Barbara Aitken was very different. Her stiff upright figure matched her character.

As for the Girls, they rarely felt they could communicate with her:

> You couldn't get through to Miss Barbara. She was wonderful and we loved her to death but she was a great disciplinarian. Also there was a shyness, probably she thought she daren't get too close.

Now with her improved status she stopped being lively and vivacious and became austere. She appeared to have no personal life; only once was she seen with a man and that was during the Popplewell season when an extremely dignified older man visited her. The Girls respectfully noted, 'That's Miss Barbara's gentleman friend.' Apart from that sole relationship no one ever talked about a man friend. Mr Smith drily observed in retrospect, 'She may have had her wild moments at times. I don't know for sure, but I doubt it.'

Barbara went to live with Doris in Putney; the war years were still times when two women could set up home without gossip. Just as Doris had made the organization her whole existence with Mrs Tiller, now the same pattern was repeated with Barbara. They constantly worried about whether the Girls were really behaving themselves, so much so that the weekly report was initiated. From now on the Head Girl was instructed to write a weekly letter about her charges. So seldom did anything go wrong, that rather like a penitent without sins at confession, the Head Girls' reports dwelt on trifles. The fact that a certain person did not hang her stage clothes properly would assume enormous importance. To a certain extent their friendships were vetted; it was noted who they spoke to and any friendships with other artistes in the show were definitely frowned on. The Girls began to suspect that everything they did and said was going back to the Firm — and it was.

There was the usual dilemma about boyfriends; no one knew the actual ruling but dared not risk the Captain's wrath by going above her and asking the Misses D and B outright. The Head Girl's interpretation was Law. Some gave orders that there were to be no dates whatsoever. This totally unrealistic command was broken by meeting men surreptitiously well away from the theatre. The Girls patronized the coffee bars inside the cinemas. There they could relax confidently with the servicemen knowing that if they were caught by a strict Captain, they could pretend they had been obliged to share tables.

Most of the younger ones were frankly overawed by men. One Girl is touching whilst expressing her fears in a diary:

> Larry came over. Eighty miles by car. He was so annoyed because I wouldn't go out with him. He was quite persistent and frightened the life out of me. I've made up my mind I never want to see him again but he said he can always find me through listings in *The Stage*.
>
> Another entry: Frank scares me, he is so persistent. I have an idea he is a wolf but he'll have to change his plans as he is not getting me.

Despite youthful fears and puritanical rules, love did blossom. News of any romance had naturally already reached the Firm via the weekly report but when it got to the serious stage of getting engaged, Miss Doris would take on the parental role and say rather regally, 'Well dear, we would like to see him. What does he do?' The girl had an uncomfortable feeling that if her fiancé was in a job considered unsuitable, somehow the relationship would be nipped in the bud.

Because of the shortage of trained dancers available, married women were now accepted for work. Any Head Girl having proved her abilities in the past was welcomed back. However unfortunately for the women who married men in show business, wives were not allowed to work in the same show as their husbands. This was utterly frustrating. Often they had first met working together yet now they were expected to work apart. The fact that Doris and Barbara were not specific only confused matters. The husband would sign his contract for a production, hearing that a Tiller line was also booked for the show. His wife would then rush into the Tiller office and ask to be in that troupe and the answer would inevitably be 'No' and an offer made miles away from him. The poor bride had an impossible decision to make, either to work far away with the Tillers or to give up dancing and travel with him.

When the Girls joined in the victory celebration nights all over the country, they shared a nationwide feeling that life would change for the better. In most ways it did not. Rationing continued and became even more severe at one point. Was this the wonderful new world they had been fighting for? Military service had changed many men and women who often found it difficult to adjust to civilian life. Family tensions arose and reality was difficult to live with. But dancers were lucky. They could escape. Away from home, the Tiller world continued as usual. For the past sixty years they had described how they felt about each other: 'We were just like sisters.' The war had not changed that but strengthened the bond between all the dancers who worked during that time.

9

'Send Me Where I'll Be Most Useful'

Touring could be fun by the seaside

ONCE THE war had ended, variety artistes serving in the forces were impatient to get back into show business. Old ties between the Tiller name and Blackpool were re-established when they were offered the summer season booking. It was for George and Alfred Black at the Opera House. These two men loved the entertainment business with all their hearts and every year they mounted an ambitious programme. At last the Girls revelled in the luxury of new stage costumes. There was no more racing to beat the others to get to a skip of well-worn costumes. To complete Tiller bliss, new shoes were provided for each routine.

Blackpool, friendly as ever, welcomed the entertainers and provided a wide choice of amusements for them in their spare time. Not only were the performers from the numerous theatres able to meet up at charity functions such as football matches and fêtes but there was dancing in the ballrooms after the shows into the early hours with the musicians from the big orchestras, Joe Loss, Ted Heath and Geraldo after they had finished their set.

There was a second Tiller line working at Blackpool at the North Pier. This was for Lawrence Wright. It had an important link in their history as this famous music publisher had been a close friend of John. There was a little envy from these Girls; after all the Opera House was the pinnacle of show biz. Because of his past association with John, Lawrence was allowed first choice of his line of Girls and if he took a fancy to a particular Girl, he would get her. She would never be able to escape from his contract, everyone in the office was at such pains to appease him:

> I was dying to get onto the Opera House stage but the old devil kept choosing me. Three years I was stuck with him, then he died and that was the end of that booking. At last I was able to achieve my ambition.

One summer a new singer was booked – Frankie Vaughan. Either his manager or Lawrence thought of a scheme to create a sensation at every performance. All the Girls were told to put on their outdoor clothes, sit in the audience and scream during his act. The self-effacing Tillers were terribly embarrassed at doing this but of course dared not refuse. It was bad enough when people turned round and tut-tutted but, worse still, they knew the audience would guess that it was a publicity trick; their stage make-up was too obvious and their empty seats for the rest of the show provided absolute proof. When the press published the story they were not asked to continue the farce.

There were many successful impresarios creating work after the war. Emile Littler still had his empire at Pantomime House, Laidler continued in Yorkshire and the well-known entrepreneur Jack Hylton booked a Tiller troupe for every *Crazy Gang Show*. However, he and most of the Gang had such reputations as womanizers that their notoriety had even reached the genteel ears of the Firm. Early in rehearsals Barbara gathered the troupe together in the stalls of the Victoria Palace. She solemnly warned the Girls, who felt that her lecture was an insult in that the men were all so physically unattractive! As Jack Hylton was only around for rehearsals, he had a limited time to make a pounce. He, too, was regarded quite cynically but they always felt reasonably safe as he usually had a mistress watching all rehearsals.

The Gang were famous for playing tricks on their colleagues, on and off stage. This was uproarious for the audience but could cause nervousness amongst the professionals who were geared to present a perfectly drilled act. A single or double act could improvise round a situation but not nineteen dancers trying to protect an unfortunate friend. Shoes placed in the wings in readiness for a quick change were nailed to the floor whilst the Girls were dancing on stage. Coloured lumps of dough were thrown at them from the wings which was embarrassing for the sensitive but it seems the egotists felt proud to be chosen!

Either the practical jokes unsettled the Girls or maybe it was simply the long length of the runs of the *Gang Shows*, but they certainly became more accident-prone at the Victoria Palace. A busby gradually slipped over one Girl's eyes until she was totally blind for the remainder of the routine and the ultimate nightmare of female performers actually occurred to another. Both her dress straps broke. She completed the number with her arms across her chest holding her dress up as best she could. She certainly deserved most of the applause that night. Then show titles seemed to invite gremlins: garters kept falling down during the run of *Knights of the Garter* and many a head was banged by the bells as the Girls made their first entrance in *Ring Out the Bells,* the show put on in honour of the coronation.

A contract at the Victoria Palace meant financial stability for at least eighteen months. In addition to their salary of £7, there were often cabarets at the big hotels earning them an extra £2 a performance. For the same salary a more exciting life was enjoyed by the Girls at the Palladium. There the management had a policy of booking the great international stars of the time. What they gained in morale by mixing with Danny Kaye, Dean Martin and Jerry Lewis, they certainly repaid in rehearsal time, especially if the show only ran for two weeks. Naturally the most popular stars were booked for longer runs.

Union membership was compulsory in the London theatres and as Nessie Tierney, the admirable Equity organizer, trudged round the West End shows collecting subscriptions, she tried to make the dancers aware of the benefits of belonging to their trade union. They were grudging with their money and when she turned up with a banner and pleaded with them to join in a picket for a rise of from £8 to a minimum of £11 for chorus workers, she got no support at all. They had been indoctrinated into believing that their only allegiance was to the Tiller organization, and their blinkered thinking allowed them to believe that any militancy with wage claims for Equity would be bad for the Firm when negotiating contracts. They were on the minimum salary anyway, a far cry from John Tiller's day when he paid well above the average. The chorus dancers' fight was won by the union and when working in the West End, the Girls gained by the efforts of their more courageous peers.

Fewer used the Theatre Girls' Club now. The spartanism of the place was definitely too dreary for any lengthy stay. Time had stood still. The front door had numerous locks and bolts to be undone each time it was opened. Immediately a Girl had come inside, it would be noisily locked up again. To add to the jail-like atmosphere, there was the sight of Miss Bell, in charge since the twenties, walking about with her enormous bunch of keys round her waist. However it was excellent value at only thirty shillings a week.

Bert Hardy recorded the spartanness of the Theatre Girls' Club where the Girls learnt a few facts of life (BBC Hulton Picture Library)

The perky Poodle Parade

The fifties were the heydays of prostitution in Soho and this provided the best pastime of all at the Club. Outside on the street at regular five yard intervals, women, sometimes with a small dog, would linger. The Girls could hardly wait to finish their meal and race upstairs to watch business being transacted. Some timed the women as they disappeared down the alleys. The record? Three minutes, inclusive of departure and return! One new Girl waited on the corner of Dean Street for her friends to catch up with her. After at least ten men had approached her asking the time, a furious voice shouted 'Are you aware, ducky, you're on my pitch?' She wanted the ground to swallow her up.

Non-Londoners appearing at West End theatres faced great difficulty getting accommodation. Once a long-running show had opened, only the weekly brush-up call was considered necessary. It was extraordinary to feel entirely free every day for months on end. During summer season shows, the Girls had always met up each morning to collect their post, have coffee and go off in small groups to the beach or the cinema. London was so vast, it dispersed them. With everyone living in different parts of the metropolis it did not seem worth travelling long distances to meet. Hanging around for hours waiting for the evening show cost too much money.

This loneliness was partly responsible for a couple of victims succumbing to anorexia, a disease that began to appear in the fifties. Non-medical people had no idea of the symptoms or cause. Therefore it was not surprising that no one in the Tiller office knew how to deal with a really serious case that developed. The Girl concerned was exceptionally attractive with a sweet and gentle personality. She originally joined a Tiller troupe in pantomime to get enough money to pay for her ballet classes, shoes and clothing. Her priority in life was to pass her teacher's examinations. With this in mind she accepted a summer season at Blackpool. When the classes held there did not improve her technique as much as she expected, she did a workout in the theatre on her own every morning.

When the show transferred to London in the autumn she took a flat with another Tiller, who was so involved with a new boyfriend that the flat-mates rarely met. Returning to an empty flat at night was depressing but the free time during the day did not bore her. In London there were so many classes with high standards; she went to a couple every day. She loved classical dance and soon realized that Tiller dancing was not what she wanted in life. It became impossible to budget for meals and classes:

I couldn't afford to eat and go to classes. I didn't starve, just cut down on food, so I thought. In the morning I would only have a cup of coffee and then go to a class. In the afternoon I would decide to have a cup of coffee and go to class instead of eating lunch. By teatime I was past eating, you don't want to have a big meal before two shows anyway, so I would have another cup of coffee and something small like a Welsh rarebit. Then after two shows I was too tired to cook, just had another cup of coffee and went to bed.

Because I knew by then Tiller work wasn't for me, I started auditioning for better contracts, even for the Festival Ballet, that was really what I wanted, but by that time I'd dwindled down to six stone.

Still dancing at well below six stone, the climax came when Doris became alarmed about the effect her emaciated body would have on television viewers in a forthcoming programme and ordered her home. Down to four stone, she was put into hospital. After months of patient work with her doctor, she finally started to put on weight. It was many years before she had conquered the disease.

Dancing was her priority to the point of obsession but it had become increasingly important for all dancers to improve their standards. When *Oklahoma* was brought over from America in the late forties, it made a tremendous impact, and *West Side Story* even more so later on. As far as the Girls were concerned, they were proud to continue to go through their highly distinctive routines but at the same time, many were eager to dance in the new American style.

The problem was how to acquire the skill. London had many of the finest teachers of ballet in the world but there was a distinct lack of modern dance classes. The only answer was to get into a show that had the new choreography. Unfortunately almost all the Girls had been Tillerized and knew it. They even lacked the courage needed to try the open auditions where hundreds of aspirants competed for a dozen places. There was a solution if they were booked for the big shows when an outside choreographer was employed to arrange the production numbers, then they got work to stretch them.

Unfortunately the choreographers they worked with were not the greatest in the country, let alone the world, and probably because they were aware of this, they were often bitter and sarcastic. George Carden, who dominated the Palladium shows, was the worst culprit. At the other end of the scale was Lionel Blair. He was adored, his joy of dance being infectious, apart from his charming way of talking to them as individuals. It was fascinating to people who had been told to think collectively.

While the Palladium was in its greatest era in the 50s, the Girls worked with all the international stars (International News Photos)

133

Joan Davis undoubtedly made the most lasting impression of all their choreographers. This was obviously her intention as she was outrageous:

She looked 'butch' for a start, which was frightening. If you were new, she would take you by the hand, walk you to your place and kiss you on your cheek. Though we were green, we got the message.

She put the fear of God into all of them. Some desperately changed their hairstyle to one they imagined she liked, anything to get on the right side of her, but nothing could change this woman's mind. She took an instant liking to some and an absolute hatred to others. These she would order to dance behind the largest pillar on stage.

Yet to a painfully shy girl who went to the back row of her own accord, Davis would pause, smile at her, beckon and say, 'Come on dear, yes you, right down to the front row.' If they were too close to another dancer, she would embarrass them by saying 'Get out of that Girl's knickers.' She repeatedly told them that their Tiller line was only there to supplement that cast, no matter how high their billing.

During the war there had been no chance of work outside Britain but now they were back in demand abroad.

Like all the women of the time, they took care in preparing and matching their outdoor clothes. The frilly petticoats took an hour to iron. The foreign press often called them a troupe of Princess Margarets because of their lady-like appearance (Keystone Press Agency Ltd)

In Denmark they were booked for the Circus Revue in Clampenborg. Barbara was dismayed to discover that the theatre consisted of a tent with wooden huts provided as dressing-rooms. 'Spit and Sawdust,' she muttered. In fact the tent was a superb marquee and served its purpose admirably. Much more of a problem was finding transport to get to it. Set in the heart of a deer park, far away from the digs, the only solution was to hire bicycles. So regularly every morning and evening, the twelve Girls would ride along in double file, Barbara in the lead, sitting bolt upright.

Nobody objected to such an agreeable way of travelling with beautiful trees lining the route; it was an admirable way of unwinding after a long hard day. Following the opening night, Barbara returned to London. Soon after this the Girls realized that while they were taking in the fresh air there was a flasher on the tree-lined route:

Eventually we decided it would have to stop. We would catch him and teach him a lesson. We pedalled along, then just like one of our routines, we stopped together on one count, dropped our bikes on the second, then we let rip. We chased after him, screaming at the top of our voices all the time. I don't know where the fella disappeared to but we didn't catch him; thankfully he never appeared again.

Barbara had laid down extra rules for the troupe going to Sweden: they must not talk politics and were never to try schnapps. As usual they had no interest in politics anyway but the taboo on the drink was tantalizing. They were reminded again not to talk politics when they went to South Africa. During the entire six months they received the same generosity and lavish hospitality as their forebears had in the 1910s and 20s. Although their wages were comparatively low, which meant they had to stay in fairly shabby hotels, their life-styles were considerably improved with endless invitations from white South Africans to socialize.

Huge T-bone steaks were offered at every meal, even at breakfast if requested. Diamond merchants almost queued up to be Stage Door Johnnies. Life could be a complete holiday for the entire run. It was as though South Africans had not seen anything like the Girls for years, they were so desperate to mix with them.

In Johannesburg the high altitude defeated them; situated 6,000 feet above sea level they were bewildered when they first found themselves breathless halfway through their routines. They were grateful for the two weeks' rehearsal time to get acclimatized.

Apart from the United States and the Soviet Union, Tiller Girls were now appearing in every country that had been conquered by their forebears at the turn of the century. So many producers were clamouring to book them, the Firm could now give continuous work to scores of Girls but they had to be willing to toe the line which began to rankle as they reached their mid-twenties. Serious relationships seemed to be deliberately wrecked by the simple method of never letting couples work together. If she heard someone was engaged, Doris would still ask the man's occupation. The reply 'comedian' was heard more often now; it was not well received as a comic's jokey and informal manner was not to her liking. One Girl had a contract cancelled without any reason given when

Doris realized she would be working with the same famous comedian who had escorted her to expensive clubs during the previous season.

Life was just like the army. They had to be prepared to go where they were sent at a moment's notice with no questions asked. Yet unlike the army, the rules were not defined. If they dared query why they were being sent somewhere, all that was said was 'That's where we need you.' Girls that showed they thrived on obedience did the best:

Miss Barbara called me into the office and said, 'You have a choice of work, the Palladium, South Africa or the Adelphi.' I was bowled over and said, 'Send me where I'll be most useful.'

The result was that Vivienne Race eventually worked in all three places! So it was obviously in their interests to obey and they were aware of their submissiveness:

In just two shots Bert Hardy brilliantly captured the atmosphere backstage: waiting to go on, and the mad rush to clear the wings once the number is finished (BBC Hulton Picture Library)

We were so subdued, we had to be like sheep to work as Tillers. During a lull in a rehearsal when nothing seemed to be happening for ages, we all stood around. After quite a while one person might sit down, and then we would all gradually follow suit. I used to go 'Baa...Baaa.'

Although variety acts, as they become more successful, could and did refuse dates in second-rate theatres, Tiller Girls could not. It was bad enough to go back to well-worn costumes and ill-fitting shoes after a West End run but many English provincial theatres were still ill-equipped, unhygienic and cold. The number of wash-basins in the dressing-rooms had not increased even though the numbers in the troupes had. Rats were often a problem but at least when they were at a certain Leeds theatre, the night watchman did provide a diversion by killing them with his bow and arrow. True, his bait, a kipper in a cage did stink the place out but he was immensely proud when he was successful, summoning the entire troupe to look at the dead rat which he laid out in state on a tin tray. Then he would go back to sharpening his homemade copper-tipped arrow in preparation for the next attack.

Most theatres had a self-appointed vicar or priest who would enjoy meeting the theatricals once a week. It was much more fun for the Girls when the Mad Monk would turn up in full drag carrying a huge cross.

To be sent to work in Hanley was a fate worse than death, was the general opinion. To start with they would all try to stay in bed till mid-day as they were so bored with the town. Then the digs were usually dreary and one landlady even served the same dinner every day for the entire six-week

TILLER'S GIRLS

season: pork chop and spotted dick. Another provided such a small
bedroom that the dancers had to clamber across beds to sit down and eat
but they could hardly stomach the food because the husband delivered it
with filthy hands. At night he brought them stone hot-water bottles which
got blacker every time. To add to the grimness, one poor dancer broke
three toes tripping over a cable backstage during the pantomime. Barbara
swiftly arrived and ordered no fuss or publicity over the accident and
arranged for the Girl to sing in the chorus so that no compensation could
be claimed.

A typical Sunday Night at the London Palladium

Despite the bad dates, the Tiller standard was flying as high as John
would have expected. They appeared in the comparatively new medium of
television. How he would have thrived mentally as well as financially at
the challenge. *Sunday Night at the London Palladium* undoubtedly re-
established their fame. It was transmitted at prime time on Sundays for so
many years that little girls watching it at tea-time were eventually able to
achieve their ambition and join the line. Like most light entertainment on
TV at the time, it went out live with an audience, which was excellent for
getting the adrenalin going but stressful. Not only were there over 2,000 in
the Palladium audience but relatives and neighbours were amongst the
millions watching in front of television sets. They knew the exact position
their Girl was dancing, so the slightest mistake became a nightmare. As it
happened, Girls chosen for the early shows were so experienced that they
rarely made an error but there was always the fear of doing so.

Rehearsals were brief. The routine would be learnt on Thursday
morning followed by costume fittings. Then rehearsals all day Friday and

138

half a day Saturday. Straightforward kicking numbers were most popular with the public and with this in mind and in order to cope with such short rehearsal time, the shorthand noting of steps was useful. Just by muttering 'knock, knock' or 'muscle', which described a particular set of steps lasting around four bars of music, any Girl with a couple of seasons' experience could be talked through a number at a moment's notice. Cameras challenged precision so the height of the kicks was lowered to just above the waist.

Sunday was a long, tiring day starting at 10 am. Girls sitting in the stalls waiting for their turn on stage were so nervous that they hardly enjoyed watching the stars rehearse. Each one reacted to the strain in a different way. Normally happy-go-lucky ones could be seen marking out the routine every possible minute. Some almost chain-smoked while a few shook and others came out in blotches.

Pills and tranquillizers were given without hesitation by GPs at the time and a few found that the odd one helped to cope with the recording day. They loathed being distracted by having to stand in for the public in a run through of the *Beat The Clock* games, their main concern being to concentrate on their routine with no wish for the unwelcome honour of presenting the prizes.

It did not seem to dawn on those in authority that Tiller Girls were dancers and not static figures. Fairly regularly someone had the stupid idea of sewing diamantés onto their fishnet tights so that if a Girl's leg came into contact with another the two legs got entwined and wrenching apart the tights would tear leaving a sizeable hole. Often head-dresses were inadequately mounted and would waver during the dance. Neither Doris nor Barbara dealt with the problems; it was as though they were frightened to create any friction.

The extra tension created by the TV network was responsible for bringing a highly important person into their lives – 'Dib Dibs'. It was thought that this personage, a cross between a saint and a fairy godmother who leant towards the masculine gender for some reason, would look after all the Tiller Girls on special occasions such as opening nights and all television programmes. Forming a circle, their Captain would start off with what can only be described as a prayer, 'Dear Dib Dibs, please make us keep the line straight' and the rest of them would repeat the request; whatever the Captain said, they repeated. At the end they did a small curtsy. After this homage it was back to the dressing-room for a few more cigarettes, mark through the routine again, find even more blotches until the tannoy summoned them down to the stage.

To this day simply humming the Palladium signature tune can bring out the goose pimples. Their starting position was inevitably the same, at the back of the stage facing the audience with the front curtains closed. What added to the tension was being able to see the television monitors in the wings. The end of *The Saint* and the commercials seemed to flash by, then as the curtains were shown on the screen, their stomachs sank, they were behind those same curtains, at the same time their brains going through the routine. There was a countdown from stage management: 10-9-8... just like blast off. Minds became blank, the curtains swooped back and they were off like rockets, kicking straight down towards the massive audience, strong lights blazing on them. With no footlights, the sloping stage floor seemed like a sheer drop into the cavern that held over two thousand applauding people. Throughout the routine their minds were split, concentrating on the steps and revelling in the experience: 'I'll never forget this, how can I hold on to this a bit longer', 'It's the most wonderful time of my life'. Whatever their thoughts, the applause continued throughout the routine and so did the smiles. Normal breathing was out of the question: they almost held their breath for the entire three minutes. Suddenly it was over. They knelt and accepted the final wave of applause and kicked off. As they reached the wings gasping for breath, tension released, their first act was always to unzip each other, the costumes by now seeming so tight.

There was always someone wanting to get away from it all!

Naturally at home their parents were determined to see the show but many did not own TV sets so they scrounged invitations to neighbours' homes or even watched in a pub. Relatives and neighbours proudly placed photographs of their Girls on top of the set yet at the same time their appearances produced an extraordinary reaction from some of them:

My aunty lived in the same street as us, she would say to me, 'Saw you on TV last night, it was fantastic.' I found out years later she would say to my mother, 'I don't know why your daughter doesn't get a decent job.' Several women said to mothers, 'Why are you letting your daughter do that job?'

Yet they all loved watching the Palladium show and took pleasure in boasting to their friends that they knew one of the performers.

Tillers were booked every other week. During their week out some took quite ordinary jobs. One Girl at Woolworths was asked for her autograph when the other assistants found out. Mr Smith and Barbara, not seeming to understand that they could not live on one week's salary for a fortnight, were quite shocked to hear that some Girls signed on at the Labour Exchange, as they were legally entitled to do.

Not one Girl broke down under the strain of TV work. Barbara seemed to thrive on it, avoiding any personal confrontation with those in charge by never querying alterations to her routines. Doris, as always, remained a tower of strength to everyone around. With her lovely round smiling face she welcomed the affection the Girls felt for her and which they openly displayed. Hugs, pecks on the cheeks, linking arms, friendship was so easy with Doris whereas no one would have dared touch Barbara.

When Mr Smith and Doris went on various trips around the country to see their troupes in action, he never ceased to be amazed at the number of telephone calls she made in every town as there were so many ex-Tillers she still kept in contact with. In reply to the dubious weekly report no fewer than ten Captains a week were sent affectionate letters, often handwritten in warm, rounded script. She and Barbara still lived together and 'Tiller talked' into the early hours. Mr Smith regarded this as unnatural. He was determined that when work was over, unless he had to visit a theatre, he would go straight home to his family in the summer months dead on the dot of 5.30 every evening and spend a few hours gardening. Just as loyal as the others but firmly resolved to separate himself from what he realized could become a hotbed of pettiness, he still steered himself away from the dancers, corresponding only with the 'skipper', as he preferred to call the Captains, over wage sheets and national insurance deductions.

Despite his reticence it was surprising that quite a few Girls asked his advice on marital problems, particularly a potential divorce. When they arrived, he would close up his ledger and walk round and round Leicester Square with them talking through the problem. Even if the husband was beating up his wife, his advice was usually to stick with the marriage as he held married life in such high esteem. He was saddened that some of the Girls remained spinsters.

When Doris herself asked his opinion about an offer of marriage, his advice was to accept. This reply was based on a few facts that the Girls did not know. Outside the Firm, Doris did not have a single close friend. It seemed tragic to him that a woman who was so warm and caring had no one to go on holiday with. She would spend that time cycling alone or visiting the troupes, just passing time. But most of all when giving his answer he took into account that for the past two years Doris had suffered from depression. It had been severe enough for her to seek help from a psychiatrist. Life seemed so impossible at times that she not only had to take time off work but spent spells in nursing homes. Truly desperate for a cure, she even had the electric shock treatment that was prescribed in those times.

Doris Alloway (left) at home with Barbara Aitken

None of the Girls had any inkling of the depth of her sadness; only a couple of the more sensitive even noticed some nervousness at stressful times. She always wore her mask of cheerfulness and they took for granted that all was well. The stream of apparently happy letters was always sent, and she explained her absences from the office as due to bouts of phlebitis. Examining her letters with hindsight, the ones written during her depression are more determinedly cheerful than the rest.

Doris had known her suitor, Tommy France, for years. He had worked in an office underneath John Tiller's way back in the twenties. He knew the gravity of her problem and being a gentle, caring man could deal with her at her lowest ebb. They had a registry office wedding and a small reception afterwards. None of the Girls were invited but were overjoyed when the news was announced. The couple decorated a room and called it Miss Barbara's room and always welcomed her into their home.

Doris's stability and happiness only lasted a month before she had a breakdown. Although she recovered, nine months later she was so bad

142

that her husband stayed in the house with her all the time. Even when she recovered, he arranged that when he was out, Barbara should visit, literally taking over in relay. Unfortunately one day Barbara was delayed. Getting into the house with a hidden key she found that poor Doris had gassed herself.

There never had been any suicide threats or attempts that anyone knew about. In a pathetic note to her husband, she thanked him for being kind and patient throughout difficult times and said she feared being a burden to him. The handwriting was not the warm, rounded script any more, but disjointed. She had only been married nine months.

In the 1950s suicide was not only considered sinful but was illegal so the truth was withheld from the Girls. A few had relatives who, knowing her married name, spotted a small paragraph in a local paper. There were so many deaths by self-inflicted gas poisoning that it only warranted a small space. There was no doubt that the desires stated in John Tiller's will hung over her too heavily, and she paid a very high price. Now, in more enlightened times, it seems a pity that by keeping the matter a secret, the Girls did not share the lessons to be learnt from her life — or her death.

10

'What's Happening?'

'**B**Y GOD, you've got to be strong in wind and limb for this game,' remarked one Head Girl to a journalist, irreverently summing up how many felt about their work now. Miss Barbara and the stalwarts still dancing from the fifties were horrified at such outspoken remarks. To them it seemed that young women became difficult to handle the moment the bells rang in the New Year in 1960. She even made a slightly critical comment which was quoted in the newspapers:

> I've noticed that today's Girls don't have the stamina the Girls had years ago, but they're slimmer and better educated.

They were slimmer and coincidentally anorexia disappeared from their ranks. Naturally they were better educated than their predecessors; their schooling had not been interrupted by a war nor had they spent months away from home on long theatre tours which had been equally disruptive for the children of the twenties and thirties.

It was partly Barbara's fault that they had less stamina. She took for granted her own extraordinary staying power which had been built up by the hours of relentless rehearsal demanded by complicated routines. These were twice as long as the modern ones and though their kicks went past their ears they had never been puffing and blowing at the end. Doing five or nine shows a day had made them into super fit athletes. When taking control of the choreography, Barbara had cut down on rehearsal time because the modified routines were learnt more quickly, hence the comparative lack of stamina.

As for being difficult to handle, of course there was no anarchic tidal wave, but values and attitudes had been altering all through the previous decade while the Tiller régime, being so dogmatic, had not changed. The new recruits would not be tamed; they had no wish to look alike, which conflicted with the Tiller concept. If they could not see the sense behind a rule, they refused to put themselves out to obey it. For instance, the practice outfit, unchanged since the mid-thirties, looked old fashioned in their eyes, so they tried to avoid wearing it. Their rebellion did not go very far and tended to centre round the black bow tie. Rather than appear without it, a Girl during the fifties, realizing she had forgotten her precious tie, would, without hesitation although it might cost her a week's salary, take a return trip by taxi to her digs to get it. In order to stem mutiny in the sixties, most Head Girls initiated fines for any uniform violation and many a youngster was seen cutting her black belt to fake a tie rather than be hit in the pocket.

At rehearsal, and how the 60s Girls hated wearing their bowties (Associated Newspapers)

Trousers were considered smart and fashionable in everyday life but for some reason Tillers were banned from wearing them. As usual a newcomer would not learn about the rule until she had broken it. One, not being telepathic, fell foul of Barbara:

We were due to have a band call for a cabaret at the Dorchester. Because I thought it would be indecent to kick my legs up in a smart skirt or dress, it seemed sensible to me to wear trousers. Barbara just looked at me as though I was a maggot coming out of a cheese. 'Never trousers at the Dorchester,' she said. Hoping to be sarcastic back, I replied, 'What about the Ritz?' 'Nowhere,' was her answer. Unbelievable! Here we were in the sixties, skirts were halfway up women's bums in the street yet she thought trousers were indecent.

Wherever they performed, Barbara was insistent on a certain hair length for them all: collar length. If they were irritated by having to wear the practice outfit, they seethed against the compulsory hair length. In order

145

to enforce the rule, there was a specific paragraph in their contracts. She
had the annoying habit of walking behind them, tweaking the back of
their hair and ordering in true sergeant-major fashion: 'Have that hair
cut!' They became particularly nervous that their head-dresses might
topple whilst on screen during the Palladium TV show:

> There we were, elastic under our chins and about sixty hair grips to hold
> the damn things on. Oh, the glamour of it all!

Lacquer became everyone's best friend as it seemed to solve most
problems:

> If your hair moved an inch at rehearsals for TV, Miss Barbara would
> come up behind you with an enormous can of lacquer and go slosh on
> to your hair, terrifying if you didn't know she was behind you. She
> sprayed so heavily, our hair became like a board and stuck to the head-
> dress. Once I couldn't get it off. Of course we all believed the story
> about the woman who died from a sting by a bee caught in her
> lacquered hair.

Whilst no one ever won a fight over the bow tie or trouser issue, the hair
dictate was different as it encroached on their daily lives. Very few had a
good enough technique to get into the West End musicals, so because
Barbara could offer work on TV and in West End revue variety shows, the
dissidents stayed on and tried to change the Tiller system. Of course they
were unsuccessful, uniformity and discipline being the foundation of the
Tiller style; take that away and they would be the same as any other line in
the provinces. Being strong-willed, they created such friction at times that
by the late sixties, a troupe could be split into two factions with very little
respect for each other.

The trouble-makers knew nothing about the tragic loss of Doris from
the Firm and the particular effect it must have had on Barbara who found
life difficult. With only Mr Smith to confide in, and he reluctant to enter
into disciplinary affairs, it was a tedious time for Barbara Aitken.

To add to her weariness, she began to have serious problems with her
legs, so from the ranks of senior Head Girls, Sylvia Blake was introduced
as 'Miss Barbara's legs'. She had served an apprenticeship for many years
and was the perfect choice as second in command. She was so businesslike
that not one Girl ever accused her of favouritism or attempted any tricks.
The fact that she never pulled rank was the quality that impressed the
youngsters. It really annoyed them if someone aged twenty-six or so
expected respect simply because of seniority.

The new demand for equality threatened any autocratic Head Girl to
the point of feeling under siege. From the audience's point of view, they
did not fail in their job and miraculously the routines appeared as slick as
ever but behind the scenes it was a different matter. If any airs and graces
were affected they were seen through:

> Speaking to our Head Girl was rather like entering the royal presence.
> When it was time to go down to the wings, she would rise to her feet as

though she had been summoned from above. 'Going down now, ladies,' she would announce and we would clatter behind her either mimicking her or acting as vulgarly as we could.

If a newcomer was promoted to be Captain without common consent, it could prove hellish for the poor unfortunate:

I was only nineteen and got just £2 extra for doing the job. I had to call the weekly rehearsal and go to the bank beforehand for their money. When I arrived at the theatre, they were dressed in their outdoor clothes; they said that they had already done a rehearsal and would not do any more. They absolutely refused. What could I do? I had to send for Miss Barbara to come up to Blackpool.

Jan Wright was one Captain who knew how to deal with them; she simply spoke to them in their own language. It was her forthright comment on the need to be sound of wind and limb for the job. She had a store of remarks that reporters could not wait to use: 'we only do it for kicks,' 'the only peers we know are at the seaside', 'only if you're dead can you be excused from dancing', and a most deflating assessment of the Stage Door Johnnie's character: 'anyone who stands around a stage door is bound to be undesirable, stands to reason, doesn't it? Any bloke under thirty with a bit of money to splash around is bound to be fixed up already.' If the Girls were not smiling when they danced, she would mutter out of the corner of her mouth, 'Smile, you bugger', and they did!

The Firm conscientiously tried to meet every one of the hundreds of dancers who wrote in for work. As there were very few dance studios for hire, auditions were held in the Tiller office which was not only small but carpeted. Mothers and daughters, dazzled by the troupe's work on TV, were always surprised at the ordinariness of the set-up. Was this really the organization behind the world-famous Tillers?

The audition was hilarious. Me and me mum went up nine flights of stairs. Now who the hell does an audition in an office? I'd done auditions in strange places but never in a four foot square room. Not only was it carpeted but cramped by a couple of desks and filing cabinets. There was Mr Smith, Miss Barbara, Miss Sylvia, me and Mum. Oh, it was quite a little gathering. Someone said, 'Change behind that curtain, dear.'

Mr Smith looked up from his ledgers and said, 'Oh, she's a bit tall.' He seemed quite concerned about that so I tried to shove myself down a bit. Miss Barbara was wittering on that she needed some 'end girls' — a phrase I was to hear later with considerable dread. At the time it meant nothing. I angled my body to do the necessary kicks and splits — no mean achievement, and suddenly I was accepted.

In Soho at the time, strip clubs were proliferating. The dancers did not get a square deal for their heavy schedule, their life was tacky and many would have preferred to get into the mainstream of theatre dance. It is unlikely that Miss Barbara would ever knowingly have accepted anyone with a background like that but one such performer did manage to get past :

We not only did five shows a day at the club but some eight numbers in each show. We had no idea what show we were doing, just going through it over and over again with no meal breaks. It was so badly directed you were often expected to appear in two consecutive numbers but fortunately, as we usually finished each routine stark naked, it was simply a case of putting on the next outfit and joining the rest of them on stage as soon as possible. Trouble was, you wouldn't have the time to glue your nipple caps on properly and they fell off on stage, then you got fined which didn't seem fair to say the least.

It began to get very tatty, the audiences were dropping off — even to sleep sometimes. One day, an American blues singer who was there just for a week said to me, 'Listen kid, this show is going to fold, get out' — it sounded just like the films. As luck would have it, that same week Tillers put an advert in *The Stage* for a dancer. The audition was held at

Even off stage they always had to stand next to the same colleague when posing for publicity shots

Max River's Rehearsal Rooms. That place was the pits! It always stank of cats' pee and unless you carried all your outdoor clothes with you all the time thieves would nick every stitch you left around.

The other applicants seemed to disappear within a few minutes and it was down to this Miss Barbara and me. When it appeared the job was to replace someone in the new *Crazy Gang* show, I was dead keen to get it. As she was a bit snobbish, I naturally didn't mention the strip club so I pretended I had worked with the Marie de Vere troupes, and she accepted this without cross-questioning. She didn't seem to doubt my dancing ability; no, she seemed to have other doubts about offering me the job. I couldn't see why she was dithering — surely she couldn't see all those nipple caps dropping off in my past?

First she said I wasn't tall enough. To this day I don't know why I had a tape measure with me. I whipped it out, slammed it into her hand and said equally forcefully, 'Measure me'. I was amazed she did. I was the exact height. Having got over that hurdle, she seemed to want to find another excuse, my hair wasn't right. Now I knew that Tillers had short hair so quick as a flash I wrenched off the long switch I was wearing. Would you believe it? She said, 'Oh no, my Girls have perms'. Now I was desperate, surely I had reached the final stretch. 'Tell me what hairdresser they go to. I'll get it done just like them. Then can I have the job?' 'Oh I don't know,' she dithered.

Well, I took a chance. Off I went to the correct hairdresser, he made me look just like Barbara in fact. Thank goodness I did get the job, it would have been weird going back to the strip club looking like the Queen. When I did join the rest of the troupe, most of them looked quite fashionable. They were a bit suspicious of me until the damn perm grew out.

Not aware of the existence of the weekly report but shrewd enough to sense the value of silence about her erotic dance career, she let no one into the secret.

The *Pony Trot* routine was the first that had to be mastered but there were no shoes big enough to fit her size 7½ feet. The only suitable pair her Head Girl could find was a pair of Charlie Naughton's, the smallest and fattest member of the Gang.

If mistakes were made, it was customary for the culprit to apologize to the entire troupe. The older Tillers expected a grovelling 'I'm sorry, I'm sorry'. Fortunately the ex-strip club dancer made a true friend of her neighbour who would mutter to her to take no notice whenever the Captain made a criticism. Eventually she felt equal to the rest of them.

The *Crazy Gang* show was still living up to its reputation of being an accident-prone booking. At one point a replacement had to deputize for a short time. Instead of choosing someone who was out of work, Barbara drafted a Girl from the busy TV troupe. Not only was the poor dancer expected to learn about eight routines in a couple of days for this new job but at the same time was rehearsing for the TV Palladium show that week and performing two numbers nightly in cabaret. Unfortunately she was placed next to the ex-strip club dancer who had enough problems of her own trying to remember the dances herself, let alone think of muttering shorthand orders in advance for someone else:

I never got over the shock of that performance, she started doing a completely different routine! Naturally being a subservient new Tiller, I thought it must be me going wrong. Our legs were clashing against the others. The audience were all looking in our direction. 'What's happening?' I frantically asked my mentor. As usual she said, 'Take no notice'. How could I take no notice? My eyes were popping out of my head, still our legs were clashing. She never did get back to our routine. It went on and on. A nightmare. Imagine an actor saying lines from a completely different play. It gave me such stage fright. Thank goodness she disappeared after that evening. Probably went off and shot herself, poor thing.

Barbara never gave them any contingency plans. She did not expect Pony Trot bras to fall off or dancers to trip over. She set the routine and that was it. When she said exit right, they always did even if they knew they would meet up with a brick wall. Her word was absolute. Tiller Girls were not expected to think, only obey. Their 'spech' numbers inevitably ended in a kneeling position where they would wait for a count of eight to cover applause, stand, then exit right. Every night each Girl would clear into the wings by the exact same number of kicks. Not one night however. Caroline, a Girl near the centre position had fainted as she knelt and was

Unanimously voted the daftest outfit of the 60s (Houston Rogers)

lying unconscious. The right half of the troupe had exited and were standing in the wings all agog but the left half could not get past the bottleneck she created. They carried on doing the same step over and over again. Heads and kicks repeating the one step like a needle stuck in a record groove.

The two dancers either side of the victim had decided that loyalty to a friend was more important than Tiller tradition. They stopped dancing and in full view of packed house were discussing what could be done. With their arms folded they looked more like two women worrried about a bag of shopping that had split open in the street, they were so unaware of the 1,500 people in the audience.

The left half were now almost exhausted doing the same step over and over again and the conductor was waving his arms like a madman, using the incident to call them all the names under the sun. 'Go off the other way,' he kept shouting. But no, Miss Barbara had said they should exit right and that was IT as far as they were concerned.

But eventually the left half, realizing collapse was imminent, decided to test the wrath of Aitken and exited left. The stage management swept down the curtains over the body of Caroline and lifted her like a corpse. The orchestra played the music for the next sketch. By an amazing coincidence it was the Funeral March. The reaction of the audience was incredible. Their response was subdued for the rest of the show as they counted one dancer missing from the subsequent routines.

Frankie Vaughan did some publicity shots with the VP Girls, as they were known. They had not been particularly impressed when it was announced that he would be with them but his impact was tremendous. This time the Girls did not have to pretend to be hysterical fans, they were.

During a long run, musicians in the orchestra pit get to know the performers quite well and usually there is a good rapport between them. At the end of the *Crazy Gang* show there was Finale Wipe for the Girls to do. It was a routine lasting only about ninety seconds and done in front of the stage cloth while the scenery was changed for the finale. The outfit for this number was surely the daftest of the sixties: hats covered with so many feathers that the Girls looked more like roosters, calf-length dresses with slits up the front to their waists, elbow length gloves and the silliest touch of all, feather-covered handbags.

One evening the Girls were listening in their dressing-room to a song on a radio request programme being sung by one of their boyfriends. Thrilled to bits at all their names being read out, they did not notice their cue on the tannoy. Only when they actually heard the music of their dance being played did they come out of their trance. Screaming with laughter and fear at the same time, they flew down the stairs. Of course it was too late, the number was halfway through and the empty stage reflected their failure. As they took their bow in the finale, the entire orchestra stood up as one. 'Glad you could come' they shouted sarcastically. The musicians' come-uppance was not far off. The Girl who had fainted on stage was appropriately surnamed Scattergood. Her grand farewell gesture during the last week of the show was when her shoe came off, rose in the air and knocked the conductor clean out! His deputy had to nip smartly into his place. When he came to, he was not surprised to learn who had K.O'd him.

When they appeared with the Crazy Gang in the 'Young at Heart' show, the gremlins really got to work (Houston Rogers)

The first company rehearsal of any tour or summer season is usually a fairly relaxed gathering. True, there may be a slight competitiveness in the air but no great nervous tension. Unlike actors, variety artistes already have their performances rehearsed. Their main consideration is to judge how well they will get on together in the many hours off-stage. Dancers, usually prettier and more gullible than the other females in the show, found that this was the day when the men, with varying degrees, showed their predatory intentions. They were trying to stake an early claim for the season.

The so-called sexual freedom of the time was exploited by many of the men they met. Girls with the most brash, know-it-all attitudes were often quite naïve. As fame can be an aphrodisiac even to fellow entertainers, many of them could be taken for a ride. One stunning virgin really believed the top-line singer when he said he loved her. After two weeks, he progressed to the eager Head Girl who for months travelled miles across the country with him whenever she was summoned. Another singer, notorious for his penchant for really young women, could unerringly pick out the very youngest member from any line of dancers, even when sitting in the audience. A Tiller troupe was booked with him and it had two sixteen year olds. The second youngest was very beautiful so her Captain went to great lengths, putting an almost twenty-four-hour surveillance on her. Meanwhile the man had managed to have several nights with her plainer youngest charge. Her minority by two months had drawn him to her.

So-called pop stars bummed cigarettes or even cups of tea from youngsters and it was sad to see them pathetically flattered to receive scant attention in return.

One leading comedian started a relationship with a most ladylike Tiller

153

and typically of many show business affairs, although it was conducted discreetly, everyone knew about it. The only blot on the horizon as far as the others could see was that the man, although unmarried, already had a mistress. The triple alliance continued for years.

Eventually the first mistress died. Within a few months, however, the comedian had installed another mistress in his home and the Tiller Girl got second billing in his life for more than twenty years.

On sheer numbers alone, the groups were the most difficult to deal with. One Girl had strict instructions from the office when working with the most notorious:

> I had to time leaving our dressing-room to the exact minute, allowing us just thirty seconds in the wings before our number started, just in case they might be around.

Girls could end up on the couch of the self appointed 'Theatre Doctor' of a West End theatre who, at the end of their consultation, would always enquire if they had experienced an orgasm. If the answer was no, he insisted on showing them how it could be achieved.

The Tiller office still believed that their Head Girls could cope with all matters of discipline, moral and otherwise. They set great store on seeing that the really young were protected. Whether she liked it or not, anyone aged sixteen was called the baby of the troupe and the older women protected her like tigresses. A few did become pregnant but probably not a higher proportion than in other decades. One unlucky Girl, being both courageous and desperate because her mother had disowned her, told Miss Barbara of her predicament. She took her to live in her home until the Girl was able to cope. From someone they had considered austere and forbidding, this reaction surprised the others but the Girl's story was an old one and must have been heard many times by Barbara in her youth and would be repeated. What was different about the sixties' Girls was their candour; they were so open and this is what shocked the older Girls:

> Looking back I'm sure that my era didn't do half of what the established Tillers got up to but we were tactless, we chatted about who we went out with, what we did.

Nothing was too intimate to talk about; one outcome was they learned about pre-menstrual tension years before most other women. How many more mistakes were always made around that time. Periods were missed or delayed if a nervous person was rehearsing for a TV show or opening night. Sadly, many would learn that the excessive physical demands had made them more prone to infertility than the average woman.

Outside the Tiller world, life was exciting. The Beatles, Mary Quant and Biba were all gradually affecting their lives. In stark contrast, some of the dances they had to perform in the provinces were totally outmoded. As they had great humour, they were not ashamed to perform them — simply hysterical:

Undoubtedly the worst costume was for the Rose Dance. The dresses were ancient but apparently we should have felt honoured to do the Rose routine. We had this rose, a big, hard thing stuck on our bottoms and another big rose on our head. As we turned round one after another, it would get ripped off by the next dancer and dangle for the rest of the show.

Then there was the scarecrow number in which they had to tear off their tramp-like outfits to reveal stupid little dresses as though they were million dollar outfits. Unfortunately for them, the audience agreed that they looked ridiculous and roared with laughter.

One routine that simply begged for trouble in such unreverential times was the Totem Pole number. Probably revived from the distant days of the Folies-Bergère in the twenties, it was done on a blacked out stage with ultra-violet lighting. The Girls were backed in the number by the Wild Cats group who were seconded to hold a fish each. Well and truly living up to their name, they would send up the number by making their fish swim in the wrong direction knowing full well if they could make the Girls laugh, the audience would see rows of teeth lit up by the ultra-violet.

There were a great many second-rate costumes around, particularly for pantomime. Inside, the labels, grey with age, had names crossed out like second-hand school blazers. At the end of the season shoes were really scuffed and elastic bands the only method of holding them on. Tiller dancers were not sorry to see the gradual phasing out of pantomime bookings by their office.

It was becoming difficult to manage on theatre salaries; the average of £15 week by the mid-sixties did not stretch as well as before. The good theatrical landladies were either dead or becoming eccentric with age. One dear old soul still provided full board at a fair price but although four Girls were her only lodgers, she carried on laying her full complement of twenty condiment sets on the enormous dining table at each meal. They never knew whether she was expecting a last minute booking or was laying the table for the ghosts of past performers.

Manchester was a popular touring location but it became increasingly difficult to find warm digs there. When they turned up at their theatre in the morning to wash down or simply keep warm, they realized they were all in the same boat. In order to cope they took the usual depressing measures: wearing outdoor clothes and woolly hats in bed and staying there till the last minute before going to the theatre, bathing in a few inches of hot water by washing their bottom half with their top half dressed then getting out of the bath, covering their washed half and dealing with the top. Life was miserable whenever they worked there. The most important decision of the week was about Sundays, whether to invest in a train fare home or be prepared to stay for hours in a Chinese restaurant, delaying the dreaded moment of returning to the digs.

Problems with accommodation affected all theatricals across the country. The only answer was to stop searching for digs and to book flats. The Girls copied this new custom enthusiastically. Now they could choose exactly what they wanted to eat. Or could they? Many had to cook for the first time. Usually the northerners were more experienced and could intimidate the others with their housekeeping skills:

I couldn't even boil an egg. I felt embarrassed in the first place we shared. I couldn't take a turn with the cooking. I didn't like to admit I couldn't cook and was terrified they might think I was lazy and get on at me. One Sunday I decided I would do the breakfast before the others got up. I broke three eggs and threw them away before they came down. At the weekend they all did jobs around the house, all so busy, they seemed to know what was needed so I decided to clean the windows. It was freezing outside but up the ladder I went, I couldn't get the soap off and it looked terrible.

As performers trekked across the country, they knew that their profession was going through radical changes. There was no doubt that television was killing off theatre audiences. With their standard of living deteriorating, many entertainers could only see a bleak future for themselves, so they left the profession that, after the war, had seemed to promise so much.

The attitude of the Girls mirrored that of the whole profession. They could rough it with depressing digs, costumes and wages while they were young but once they reached their mid-twenties, the future was not bright unless TV work was a possibility. In that case they were openly pleased to be able to repay their parents for their childhood dancing classes. Most friends and relatives owned TV sets by this time, some even investing in magnifying glasses which hooked onto the screen and enlarged the picture but wrecked the focus if viewed slightly from the side.

At least one mother dragged her daughter round endless shopping trips to the West End, informing all the shop assistants in sight that she was on *Sunday Night at the London Palladium* while the poor girl cringed with embarrassment.

Once ITV was well established with the public, it seemed unfair to the Equity Council that a performance watched by between ten and twenty million people was paid for at a fee that was less than a week's salary in a West End theatre. There were also other unsatisfactory clauses in the agreement and when it was realized that negotiations with the programme companies were breaking down, an instruction was sent to all Equity members to accept no further engagements with commercial television after a given date.

When union meetings were held, Barbara asked a favourite Head Girl to go and report back what had been said. There was no sinister intent behind the order; she was gravely concerned about the financial predicament of the organization. The number of troupes had been allowed to dwindle to a handful so she could not absorb striking Girls into scores of troupes across the country and the world as would have been the answer in John's day. The Palladium troupe was obviously affected. There was no theatre work available, and only a handful of cabaret bookings came their way. Not having any idea how long the situation would last, many gradually found work in shops and offices.

The strike was an honourable one: members were not asked to break existing engagements, it was well supported by the Screen Actors' Guild,

the American Federation of TV and Radio Artists, Equity in Australia and
Canada and bravest of all, the small Irish Equity. Even the Press presented
the case accurately. The dispute was won in just under a year and the Girls
certainly gained, their salaries more than doubling to 28 guineas. It was
fortunate that the Equity Council had given them no choice about
striking. Even afterwards they were the first to admit that they would not
have freely done so:

> I enjoyed doing the television so much I would have done it for nothing.
> I wouldn't have gone on strike if I'd been given the choice, but I must
> admit we were grateful when we got our first pay packets and found
> almost £30. It still had to last two weeks but it certainly made life easier.

Although the lessons learned as a result of the strike should have alerted
Barbara to the dangers of having too few troupes on call, she still allowed
the fortunate TV troupe with their now reasonable salaries to take on the
best theatre work at the same time. Instead of forty dancers living off two
contracts, twenty were creaming off the best offers. Even when they
appeared as far away as Westcliffe, Bournemouth and Great Yarmouth,
they would rehearse in their theatre during the week and be transported,
often overnight, sometimes in a uncomfortable coach to London to
perform in front of the cameras on Sunday. Miraculously they managed to
smile as usual after travelling on the over-night sleeper from Glasgow
during one series.

The troupe featured in the *Sunday Night at the London Palladium* were involved in the Equity strike which stopped their high kicks for 9 months

Billy Cotton booked one such troupe for his series. After finishing in their kneeling position, they would have to scramble off on all fours out of sight of the cameras. Although their head-dresses would always get tangled up they could not give way to laughter. One Girl lost her falsies at this point. Billy Cotton may have been getting on but he was still sharp of mind and humour. After the show, he plonked the offending articles down in front of the correct Girl and said, 'I believe these are yours'.

With an ever decreasing number of 'proper' Tillers, married ones were now allowed to do TV work but without the theatre slog at the same time. This naturally caused great resentment; everyone wanted the best work but in fact the married woman was often the most experienced for the job. Girls were taken out of the Palladium line on occasions and replaced by dancers who had never appeared professionally. They were slow to pick up the steps and muttering the shorthand was no use to them. These Girls had no security of tenure as far as the Palladium show was concerned. At any point, Barbara could and seemingly did tire of them and send them off to some provincial town. For dancers this was the equivalent of being sent to the Tower or Siberia.

Every fortnight during their season in the 'Five past Eight' show in Glasgow, these Girls would travel on the overnight train to rehearse and appear on Sunday Night at the London Palladium

Poor old 'Dib Dibs' was not even liked and was soon extinct, maybe s/he should have been respected more, maybe it was an omen. The times had changed so much in the last decade. Although the Girls were still getting some excellent bookings, their popularity and Barbara's health were fading fast.

11

Finale — Wipe

Into the 1970s (Solo Syndication)

JUST AS John had caught the public's attention with his idea of absolute precision, two men now offered concepts that totally usurped the Girls as the public's favourites. The first was Robert Luff, who launched *The Black and White Minstrel Show*. On the same lines as the amateur *Minnehaha Minstrels* of John's youth, it was a full length production with the normal laws of popularity reversed, the large chorus being the stars rather than the handful of principals. The title came from the blacked-up men and white women who appeared to sing and dance non-stop. The tunes were old and familiar but performed in a way the public found exhilarating. As each song reached a climax, another would then follow to top it. The show translated well onto TV, the cameras being able to weave in and out of the dancing lines. Absolute uniformity was the aim, so naturally it was a direct competitor to the Girls' work.

159

The second challenge came from Dougie Squires. Having been a successful performer himself, he understood the desire for individuality while performing in a group, so he chose to promote dancers with their own style. Each had to have a fairly distinctive personality to get through his audition; once accepted he groomed and encouraged them to develop further. Not only were his *Younger Generation* and *Second Generation* groups popular with the public but immediately dancers saw the chance to express themselves, they wanted to work for him. It was a sad fact that the only reason most girls joined Tillers now was to get Equity union membership. Many laughed at the apparently simplistic kicking style before they auditioned but after their first rehearsal they were in as much pain as their predecessors at the turn of the century. Even graduates from the finest stage schools found agony in previously unknown muscles and were defeated within the first five minutes by the demands of shallow breathing.

Barbara was in great pain herself most of the time and although only in her mid-sixties, she suddenly looked old to them all. It amazed and naturally annoyed the regular Girls that she accepted the newcomers' lack of stamina so passively and allowed them to have plenty of breaks, merely remarking that they seemed to get tired very quickly. She never did get accustomed to their 'Hello Barbara' instead of the more formal 'Good Morning Miss Barbara' and when a photo call was set, she was utterly speechless when asked how much they would be paid.

Beside Sylvia Blake, a second pair of Miss Barbara's legs was employed: Wendy Clarke. Strictly speaking she should never have been a Tiller, being half an inch under the decreed minimum height but after an initial pantomime season it was evident that not only was her work excellent but she had the rare quality of being a good company member so Barbara saw that she got the best work available. She felt her presence was so necessary that she was willing to deviate from John's original image of level heights in the line. This presented a problem as every troupe that Wendy was to appear in had to be consequently levelled down. Over the years there was a turnover of smaller women brought in to balance her in centre position only to find themselves discarded after a few seasons, and absolutely bewildered by not learning the reason for being dropped. Eventually Wendy decided she wanted to give up dancing before it gave her up. Her pacifying nature was invaluable during rehearsals now that Barbara quickly became frustrated and irritable when routines were not working smoothly.

The confrontations of the sixties were well in the past. The seventies recruits had great affection for someone they saw as a grandmother figure. If Barbara fussed a little too much, well so did their grannies and they admired the way she would show off now and again by daintily lifting her skirt a few inches, marking the steps and showing them how it was done. Their grandmothers could not do that. It did take a little adapting to the way she persisted in calling them ladies or girls while outside choreographers yelled out 'kids' or 'darling' but it was their turn to be startled when they met up with Fred (I'll throw these chairs at you if you don't get it right) Peters.

They were so tactful that they even found a diplomatic way round the hated rule about hair length. It was simple — wigs! One daring soul put on a wig before rehearsal started. There was no comment from either her Captain or Barbara. With bated breath the others waited for a couple of days. Still nothing was said. Gradually more and more of them copied her. They were amazed themselves to get away with it; wigs were rarely naturalistic in the price range they could afford. By the time Marilyn Moss joined, it seemed as though the entire troupe was bewigged:

> When I auditioned I had very, very long hair. Not only did Barbara tell me, but it was in the contract that it should be cut short. Thinking I had to do as I was told, I had it cut. It broke my heart as I'd had it long all my life. But what really upset me was what I saw when I arrived at first rehearsal — they were all wearing wigs! Not only that, after the rehearsal, they would take them off and their lovely long hair would tumble down. I couldn't believe it.

Barbara visited the dressing-room on Opening night. While the rest of them sat complacently in their wigs, poor Marilyn knew her hair looked a dreadful mess because the new short style was impossible to cope with. Then Barbara uttered the most dreaded sentence of all: 'You'll have to have a perm'. Again Marilyn dutifully did as she was told but not only did Barbara never return again but she was stuck with short, permed hair for the rest of the season. For her there was little consolation in knowing the considerable price the others had to pay. Working in wigs could become unbearable, with enormous heat generating between hair, head and wig. Of course they dared not ask to take them off and give the game away.

The fight over fraternizing with stagehands had been won by the Girls, who were too democratic to uphold the rule anyway:

> You know me, love, I fraternize with anyone. Director or stagehand. Besides if you'd got any sense you always kept in with whoever had the kettle. Stage-door keeper, carpenter, whatever.

Quite a few stagehand husbands had progressed to better things in TV studios. That had been a great leveller as far as Barbara was concerned and helped her to accept them. Of course a few pockets of double standards remained, notably the Head Girl who had a long standing relationship with a married comedian. When she shared a flat with others, it was a case of 'Do as I say, not as I do', for she let it be known that she would not tolerate fiancés, let alone boyfriends staying with Girls in the same flat overnight. The award for devotion has to be given to one young man who, doubting that his relationship could stand the strain of continual absence, drove a total of 36,000 miles in ten months while holding down a full-time job.

Staying at the Theatre Girls' Club was more or less out of the question as its standards and residents had deteriorated so badly. One newcomer had an eye-opener to the wonderful world of show biz when she turned up to book a bed:

> I stayed at the Theatre Girls' Club; it nearly finished me off. We were on only half pay for rehearsals and I seemed to pay most of that to the

Club. It was the nearest thing to a workhouse.

My friend and I never went out at night; the training nearly killed us, our feet were raw because of the rubbing of the Tiller shoes and the fishnet tights so we fell into the place in the evening and stayed there. Living there were so-called models, a singing group, a few on drugs and all sorts of weirdos. We had a 16 stone butterfly one night, she was leaping from bed to bed.

> If you weren't up by seven in the morning, a large lady came to get you up. We smuggled food parcels in; if they caught you with them, they were most upset. Couldn't see why we needed extra food. We only got one egg a week with a slice of bread. That was at 5.30 for Sunday tea, and it had to last till Monday morning.

It was extraordinary that although none of them had ever been to public school or in the army, initiation rites were carried out on any unsuspecting person making her stage début. No one knew who started such a strange custom. Always lulling the poor initiate into a false sense of security by pretending the plan was to go after someone else, they would run a bath of cold water. Meanwhile the victim would be stripped and decorated with lipstick, talcum powder and whatever make-up was to hand. When they were satisfied with their handiwork, they pushed the Girl into the bath. After she managed to climb out, they shoved her outside the dressing-room, still naked. Nothing more would happen until the finale when they would hold onto her head-dress till the very last minute. As the idea that the Show Must Go On had been instilled into the newcomer she was more terrified about not appearing on stage properly dressed than the sadistic ritual she had just suffered.

Tiller troupes had always been booked as an act with two spots. Now producers were unwilling to pay twenty Girls' salaries for them to perform only two numbers. They were now expected to be in several production numbers and other routines besides their 'spechs'. As there were many different styles of modern dance around, each requiring a high standard of proficiency, it was an impossible demand. They were paid the Equity minimum at all times and often became bitter when they learnt that other troupes in the same town were offered £5 or £6 more.

Being in total charge of the financial side of the business, Mr Smith was well aware of the problems and predicted things would probably get more difficult. He watched and realized how hard it was to keep up standards, how frail and ill Barbara was at times and how hard it was for her to find suitable dancers. He remembered the vow he had made years ago, that he would either go on until he dropped or give up work while he had time to enjoy life. As far as he was concerned, the Tiller Girls had had a good run; for an act to last eighty-five years was against show business tradition. He decided now was the time to shed the Tiller burden. So he announced to Barbara:

> I know I'm eighty and I'm getting on but I'm still able to gad about. I have all my senses, I'm going to have a few trips abroad; I'm entitled to that.

However, if he wound up the business, there would be no work or money for Barbara. The only way round the problem was to persuade an impresario to buy the name and take the business over. He looked around, and decided that the best contender was a producer who had recently booked the Girls in Scarborough. Ironically it was none other than Robert Luff, one of the men who had precipitated their fall in popularity.

In 1973, a press conference was called to announce the take-over. The reporters observed Mr Smith was literally rubbing his hands with glee at the thought of getting shot of his Tiller job. He explained how difficult it was to deal with modern women:

> Now they can be independent and they want more and more. You say to one of them 'Go to Yarmouth', and she says, 'No I'd rather go to Blackpool. I have a boyfriend there!' Some of them even want to know who the star of the show and the choreographer is!

It was agreed that Barbara should supervise the kicking routines and Luff fought to get her better credits in programmes and television magazines than she had been given for years. There was no rehearsed troupe available when the first booking was made so general auditions were held. Some of the regulars were devastated to find themselves rejected in favour of dancers from the *Black and White Minstrel Show* who could present a more glamorous appearance at auditions.

As far as the contentious practice outfit was concerned, Luff kept the black and white image but got rid of the hated bow tie and blouse, thereby tactfully deferring to tradition but at the same time moving more with the times. At last their hair could be as long as they wished although none of this was appreciated as there were only two or three ex-Tillers in the line.

Despite the fact that they had a successful manager, there were many long gaps between bookings. There was only one more series of *Sunday Night at the London Palladium*. Mr Smith had been proved right in his judgement to sell out. In 1978 Tillers returned to the Opera House, Blackpool. For some reason the troupe was not only a particularly attractive set of dancers but the most ambitious. Opening night was delayed because the star, Ronnie Duke, suffered a heart attack. The extra rehearsal time was gratefully accepted by Barbara who had quite a few problems with her current crop. Only two had worked with her before and the rest were not prepared for the sudden agony of her training. The jargon they used to explain their injuries must have seemed like a foreign language to someone who had endured the no-nonsense approach of the twenties. Shin splints and stress fractures were a long way from Jennie massaging a suffering creature with horse oils or pouring a bottle of disinfectant on bleeding feet. Two dancers never even managed to get on stage for the Opening night and had to be replaced. In fact so many injuries occurred throughout the run that it was rare for a full team to appear. The Head Girl, experienced though she was, became hard pushed reorganizing moves to cover the constant absences caused by shin splints, bad backs, ripped muscles, diarrhoea. It was more like a casualty ward. As they took their places in the line one particular night, there were so many elastic bandages on so many legs she remarked they looked more like racehorses at the starting gate.

Luff did the Tiller name proud the way he promoted the Girls that season. There were publicity stunts, personal appearances, beauty competitions to judge; as they walked round with their special sashes and were pestered for autographs, they felt as famous as many of them hoped to become. On stage they loved the costumes he provided, in bikini style for the 'spechs' and at last the flattering high leglines their predecessors had craved. The dances devised by Pam Devis matched their sophisticated costumes and they enjoyed performing them but the audience response to the sight of their traditional kicking routine amazed them. They had never heard such rapturous applause before and probably wouldn't again. Of course, the loyal Blackpool audiences were not only clapping them but memories that went back years.

Although Barbara Aitken coped ably with the choreography at Blackpool that year, she was finding life wretched. She had chosen to pay for medical treatment but her illness was continuous and she was caught in the trap of paying fees beyond her means. She did not appear to have any relatives to give her any sort of support, financial or emotional, but the two women who acted as her 'pairs of legs' at rehearsals became surrogate daughters to her.

There were many tedious spells in different hospitals for her, often involving operations. At one point, Barbara was placed in a geriatric hospital which really distressed her, and she pleaded never to be sent back there once she managed to return to her flat. During each hospital visit, Wendy sat by her bedside, memories of the happier times they had shared passing through her mind. Once outside she could not hold back the tears; there seemed absolutely nothing she could do to help Barbara out of her misery. Both she and Sylvia had full-time jobs; a loyal friend from Barbara's childhood was willing to help but had suffered a stroke herself. There seemed to be no answer. Then the doctors judged that Barbara's leg would have to be amputated, a poignant sentence for someone who had been so proud of her dancing. At this point, as many Girls as could be contacted were told how badly she needed support. They rallied round well; cards, flowers and many visitors arrived in an attempt to help her through her most difficult time. At last they could express the affection she had seemed to prohibit before.

The false leg prescribed was very heavy. Putting aside her own squeamishness, Wendy would force herself to help Barbara. Although they organized a rota, chasing back at the end of the day to cook meals and do washing, the two women never stopped worrying while they were at work. They became so concerned about her being left alone for hours on end that they considered trying to pay for a nurse to help. Then there was a final blow to Barbara: she was told that the false leg she had was only temporary and that the new one would be just as heavy. It seemed that she just gave up hope. She died in October 1981.

Four days later there was a reunion for all the Tiller Girls. The two brief references in national newspapers had created a far bigger reaction than Pam Harcourt, the organizer, had imagined. Her teenage son was trying to study for examinations and both of them had to cope with an absolute barrage of telephone calls which increased as the news spread. Often the caller went to unnecessary lengths to explain her credentials, sometimes claiming to be an original Tiller Girl, which was unlikely. Usually the phrase meant they had been trained by John or Jennie. How proudly they used the word 'trained'.

National and local newspapers as well as television producers announced their intention of covering the event. It became obvious that they might dominate the day. Pam was determined that the greater part should be set aside for the women to talk together without the intrusion of cameras, so with a firmness that confirmed her past Head Girlship, she set aside a short time specifically for the media.

And so the Tillers descended on the Grosvenor House Hotel in Sheffield. They were all ages, shapes and sizes. In particular the women of the 1950s seemed heavier and taller than the rest. The tiny women of the 1920s almost got crushed. Now in their seventies, they had not shrunk with age; it was simply that women were smaller in those days. They retreated to a safe corner and it was touching to see them holding hands, trying to recognize each other after fifty years of separation. Scrapbooks and photographs were exchanged and the memories flowed: the heady times of the Folies-Bergère, views of South Africa, stars at the RKO studios, action shots from *Sunday Night at the London Palladium*. The excitement was tremendous and so was the noise. There was so much to catch up on; marriage, children, divorce, illness but above all happy times of laughter.

The memories flowed fast and furious. Naturally the more outrageous characters were the first to flash into their minds. Where was Edna Sweetmenham? Surely she would turn up. How about the time they lost her while dancing The Big Wheel on stage? It gets a bit hair-raising when the line builds up considerable momentum as it circles round, picking up more and more Girls. Edna was always a tall, strapping woman so she was always the last person to be picked up. As they swung round they lost her down the prompt box which was below floor level by the footlights but by

Edna Sweetenham on the left

the time they returned full circle, the man inside had hoisted her up and pushed her back on stage perfectly in time with the routine. She was the joker in every troupe she joined. With her broad Manchester accent and a store of one liners that attracted so many of her comedian boyfriends, she also had a mass of red hair that was constantly tangled. One Captain eventually asked, 'Why don't you look in a back mirror to comb your hair?' Which got the repy, 'A good soldier never looks behind!' Then a forthright friend tried, 'If I had your hair I'd comb it!' Not to be put down, Edna replied, 'If I had your hair I'd mow it!' How they longed to hear her comments on the gathering.

John had controlled his dancers in such a dictatorial way that, except for his son, it was almost unknown for any of his employees even to contemplate forming a rival troupe. Consequently the biggest scandal in Tiller history was not a torrid love affair but a snaffling. The *Plazas* were involved in such a snaffling just as they made their mark with their unique high-kicking style of tall Girls. Losing one dancer is a professional hazard for any manager, but losing five out of eight from the same top troupe is nothing short of disaster. What added spice to this particular piece of gossip was the fact that the culprit was not a rival manager but one of the Girls who decided to start off on her own. Here at a reunion, which after all was to celebrate the achievements of John Tiller, Leila Grafton defiantly made an appearance.

Leila Grafton (second right) was the cause of the biggest scandal in the Tiller story

Leila had been desperate to be a Tiller Girl for many years but had not dared to audition until her father died. Having at last achieved her ambition at twenty-one, she immediately found the reality difficult to live with. So much of the strict discipline seemed ridiculous to her. Being a highly sophisticated woman she was amazed that outdoor make-up was forbidden as she had been wearing it for years. She realized that her time as a Tiller was limited. She laughed during the incessant rehearsals and no one had ever dared do that. Finally Ethel sacked her. Without hesitation Leila asked the others if they would like to join a troupe she was forming. Four more of the eight agreed and that was how she began.

There was no immediate walkout. She took the addresses of those interested, assuring them she would be responsible for the cost of rehearsal rooms and costumes and she never failed to keep her promise. She realized that the Girls would be taking a risk in joining her. She had not only noticed that they felt duty bound to send money home but their reactions when Ethel berated them gave some indication of how terrified they were of losing their jobs. Obviously if they left to join her, they never could return to the security of the Tiller fold again. So with enormous respect on both sides, they started to work together. Fed up with Ethel's domineering ways, the newly formed *Grafton Girls* made sure that their rehearsals were democratic; everyone had a say in the choreography and there were never any arguments. Leila went to the top costumiers and paid for ornate costumes; she was rewarded when the others said they were far more glamorous than any Tiller outfit they had worn.

After three weeks of rehearsals they felt ready to audition with their new act. Admittedly it consisted of three routines that owed a great debt to John Tiller but they were really rather proud of it. At the end the agent kindly but pointedly asked them to show him what they had done as Tillers. So they went through their military routine. 'That's it, don't bother with what you've put together, that's all I want!' And so they toured for months with an identical Tiller routine. When finances were absolutely stable the troupe was increased to twelve. Leila always boldly advertised for ex-Tillers ensuring that they had not only all acquired the same technique but already knew the dances as well!

Looking just as elegant as she had in the twenties, Leila looked round the reunion for the woman who had given her the sack. Ethel Helliwell, the slave driver who had frightened everyone except her to death. Her name had been on everyone's lips but she was nowhere to be seen.

Although the women still living in Blackpool did not keep in touch, they always knew how their colleagues were coping. Now they sat piecing together Ethel's story. When Ethel had sentimentally claimed that she had married her childhood sweetheart they knew she was on the rebound after her final quarrel with Mangon, the impresario. She was marrying into an extremely wealthy and socially ambitious family, who welcomed her vow of never dancing again. The incredible energy that had driven her from being a walk-on in her first show to supervising dancers all over the world was now to be channelled into a life of entertaining, golf and bridge.

Showing a surprising maternal instinct, she very much wanted a child but her doctor told her conception was impossible. When her mother-in-law forbade adoption, it was her personal tragedy that she was deprived of a chance to express the warm, loving feelings that she had deep within her. In 1976 her husband Richard died. Absolutely free, she changed radically. When drinking too much, she expressed deep regrets about her life and a strange pride in being alone in life. For a person with such determination it must have been humiliating to fail to get the two things, or rather people, she really wanted in life; Mangon and a baby. Occasional glimpses of her, including a surprise appearance on the TV show *Where are They Now?* in 1979, proved she still looked immaculate and retained the deportment of a dancer. Her enormous house was kept spick and span by a daily housekeeper. When the woman left, she was alone in her mansion.

The road where she lived was called Millionaires Road by the locals. If friends called, Ethel pretended to be out so eventually they gave up trying. She repeatedly said that she had forgotten her past life yet it was impossible to escape memories of her former gregarious life-style, the windows at the back of the house looked on to the golf club where her husband had been both president and a past captain. The sprung floor in the ballroom that had been her pride and joy was polished in readiness but was never even walked on now. The house had a deadly stillness which was intensified when she began to spend all her time in one small study.

The lovely Helliwell sisters, Mabel and Ethel (left and right) dressed for their fan dance duet which was featured in ciné-variety

It never ceased to amaze the others that Ethel of the Iron Will had a twin, but she did. Alice was a lovely dancer too

Ethel's gentle sister Mabel and husband Clarrie were some of the few frequent visitors. One day her violent rage turned against them and the relationship was severed for the rest of their lives. Her twin sister, Alice, (and it had never ceased to amaze the Girls that someone like Ethel could actually be a twin), was the only one of the large Helliwell brood to have children and Ethel doted on one of her nephews. In later life Alice was increasingly withdrawn and had to be cared for in a home. At the same time Ethel began theorizing that old people should be killed off immediately they reached their seventieth birthday. She put herself into a home and the twin sisters died within three months of each other.

Millionaires Road is a windy, gusty area and there are benches for people to sit on and contemplate life or simply get their breath back. For many years a little old man would rest at one particular place quite near Ethel's house. Being small with a fairly long beard, he looked more like a garden gnome holding on to a walking stick. He would never reply if spoken to. Most would have guessed he had been a fisherman in his youth but 'he' was in fact a 'she' who had been a dancer under Ethel's direction. It was unbelievable the change that had taken place. The women who had worked with her were always startled to see her. Like them she had started in the Winter Gardens shows as a child, then had been chosen for the exhausting work that Mangon had provided in Britain and abroad.

By all accounts she had developed a temper as terrifying as Ethel's, her rages at home could be heard across the road. She refused communication with relatives. Her co-workers remember that she was a loner, never playing the fool and photographs show her lined up looking as young and pretty as the rest.

In the neighbouring town of Fleetwood was another dancer who had worked all over Europe and on Broadway and with the RKO studio. Absolutely besotted with a Frenchman, she married and stayed with him when the war broke out. Tragically he was suddenly taken away, presumably by the Nazis, and she never heard from him again. She remained in France throughout the war, then after working as a dancer in Paris, returned to England.

She began to lead a most miserable existence in a run-down prefab, so derelict that vandals, thinking the place was empty, would smash the windows and start to break in. She lived with a woman who appeared to have a strange hold over her. Drink seemed to be their only common bond. The companion would leave the prefab for hours on end to play bingo. Bedridden with arthritis, the ex-dancer was left alone with a dog that she was terrified of, cats that would mess everywhere including on her bed, her only consolation being bottles of the cough medicine which her so-called friend bought every week. She died suddenly of bronchitis. A distant cousin arranged the funeral which the strange companion attended, herself dying three weeks later, just before the bills arrived.

Ethel would talk to old colleagues on the telephone. She had no compassion when she heard the stories of these women that lived so near her, and simply denied that they had ever existed. In her will she sanctimoniously left some of her considerable wealth to the Blackpool Ladies Sick Poor Association.

Edith Whalley and her friend Dolly Ashby were reunited after 70 years

Thankfully all is not gloom and doom for Tiller Girls in Blackpool. The story of the two sisters who auditioned in mourning clothes finishes on a much happier note. Gertie Whalley worked for years in the Tiller office, before emigrating to Australia and then New Zealand. At the wonderful age of ninety-eight she is in a Salvation Army home there. Edith, the younger sister, got married. While her husband was in the war, she was able to continue dancing but he strongly discouraged her close friendship with Dolly Ashby as he imagined she might lead his wife astray, flirting with the boys. When he returned from the war, the couple opened a theatrical boarding house. Of course her favourite lodgers were the Tiller Girls. When they booked in she would stay up till three in the morning, knitting jumpers and swapping stories with them, laughing all the time.

Edith and her friend Dolly had each other's addresses for seventy-odd years; they had succumbed to the husband's jealousy because they did not dare to let them get in touch with each other until they were in their nineties, when he presumably trusted them at last. Now a widow and happily settled in a home, Edith keeps up-to-date with all the gossip of the younger Girls. She is remarkably fit, as she proves by hopping nimbly on and off her chair lift, waving like Royalty as it transports her.

Many of the Girls had longed to join an act but few had been fortunate. Among these Marjorie Tiller married and worked with Tex McLeod. The aptly named Sunny Rogers with her glorious smile initially joined a rope-spinning and sharp-shooting act called *Buck and Chick* and still works

170

as stooge to Frankie Howerd in his act. Sonia Jones became part of the brilliant Molidor Golliwog act. Then there were the enterprising *Skylarks* who all turned up to prove they were very much alive and still kicking.

As the Girls traced their fortunes it seemed that after they left the shelter of the Tiller organization it was rare for them to venture into a totally different world. When they did, their choices were fascinating whether it was Betty Boothroyd becoming an MP for fourteen years, a woman from the fifties joining the prison service or one from the sixties becoming a Moonie. Whether they were talking about a career, marriage or gossip they became so immersed with each other that they were completely uninterested in the photographers trying to record the event.

John Tiller's finest achievement was to give little girls like these a chance to change their expectations in life

In an attempt to get a photograph of the entire group, the journalists persuaded them to go out on to a flat asphalt roof. It was chaotic. After all, Miss Barbara was no longer there and although many Head Girls were present, no one had been officially nominated as the ultimate Captain. The Tiller reticence was well to the fore. Suddenly with no regard for the coarse asphalt roofing, a small plump woman went into a jumping split. At last the photographers had a focal point. They clustered round her. It was a perfect shot; she was so still and perfectly poised, she looked more like an art deco statue with her thirties bobbed hair and fringe. All the other Tillers had been deserted by the media; this was the big story. When she was satisfied they had enough good shots of her she ushered the crowd of reporters towards a place where she had arranged numerous piles of her newspaper cuttings. 'Before we start,' she announced, totally in command, 'I'd like you to know, I wasn't a Tiller Girl, but I wish I had been, it sounds fun.' Although she had no right to gatecrash the reunion because she had played no part in their history, how accurately she echoed their feelings. It really had been fun despite the hard work and pain.

One woman in her seventies, Florence Wall, had proudly brought along a large photograph that had obviously been taken from its frame. It showed fourteen little girls dancing in the street. It would be an insult to their parents to describe them as poorly dressed but without doubt they are working-class children. What is wonderful to see is the happiness and hope in their faces. It sums up how John Tiller, even after his death, was able to give ordinary little girls and women a chance to change their expectations in life. That photograph was the inspiration for this book.